Practicing Public Diplomacy

Explorations in Culture and International History Series
General Editor: Jessica C. E. Gienow-Hecht

Volume 1
Culture and International History
Edited by Jessica C. E. Gienow-Hecht and Frank Schumacher

Volume 2
Remaking France
Brian Angus McKenzie

Volume 3
Decentering America
Edited by Jessica C. E. Gienow-Hecht

Volume 4
Anti-Americanism in Latin America and the Caribbean
Edited by Allan McPherson

Volume 5
Practicing Public Diplomacy
Yale Richmond

PRACTICING PUBLIC DIPLOMACY

A Cold War Odyssey

Yale Richmond

Berghahn Books
New York • Oxford

Published in 2008 by
Berghahn Books
www.berghahnbooks.com

Library of Congress Cataloging-in-Publication Data
Richmond, Yale.
   Practicing public diplomacy : A cold war odyssey / by Yale Richmond
     p. cm.
   Includes bibliographical references and index.
   ISBN 978-1-84545-475-3 (hardback : alk. paper)
   1. United States—Foreign relations—1945–1989. 2. Cold War.
3. Richmond, Yale. 4. Diplomats—United States—Biography. 5. United States Information Agency—Biography. 6. Diplomats—United States—History—20th century. 7. Public relations and politics—United States—History—20th century. 8. United States—Relations—Communist countries. 9. Communist countries—Relations—United States. 10. Cultural relations—History—20th century. I. Title.
E744.5.R53 2008
327.73009'045—dc22   2007025072

British Library Cataloguing in Publication Data

A catalogue record for this book is available from the British Library

Printed in the United States on acid-free paper

ISBN 978-1-84545475-3 hardback

Ask not what your country can do for you;
ask what you can do for your country.
—John F. Kennedy

ADST–DACOR Diplomats and Diplomacy Series

Since 1976, extraordinary men and women have represented the United States abroad under all sorts of circumstances. What they did and how and why they did it remain little known to their compatriots. In 1995 the Association for Diplomatic Studies and Training (ADST) and Diplomatic and Consular Officers, Retired, Inc. (DACOR) created the Diplomats and Diplomacy book series to increase public knowledge and appreciation of the involvement of American diplomats in world history. The series seeks to demystify diplomacy by telling the story of those who have conducted our foreign relations, as they lived, influenced, and reported them. *Practicing Public Diplomacy: A Cold War Odyssey*, is the 32nd volume in the series. (For more information about this series refer to the ADST Web site, www.adst.org.)

Contents

Acronyms

ACC	Allied Control Council.
ADST	Association for Diplomatic Studies and Training.
AFL-CIO	American Federation of Labor-Congress of Industrial Organizations.
AFP	*Agence France Presse.*
BBC	British Broadcasting Corporation.
CBC	Canadian Broadcasting Corporation.
CEO	Chief Executive Officer.
CIA	Central Intelligence Agency.
CO	Conscientious Objector.
COMEX	Committee on Exchanges.
CPI	Cooperation with Private Initiative.
CSCE	Conference on Security and Cooperation in Europe.
CU	Bureau of Educational and Cultural Affairs.
DACOR	Diplomatic and Consular Officers, Retired.
EUR	Bureau of European Affairs.
FBI	Federal Bureau of Investigation.
FBIS	Foreign Broadcast Information Service.
FSI	Foreign Service Institute.
FSO	Foreign Service Officer.
FRG	Federal Republic of Germany.
GKNT	State Committee on Science and Technology.
GRU	Main Intelligence Directorate.
GS/YF	Graduate Students/Young Faculty.
HICOG	High Commission for Germany.
IMG	Information Media Guaranty.
IRC	Information Resource Center.
IREX	International Research and Exchanges Board.
IUCTG	Inter-University Committee on Travel Grants.
IVP	International Visitor Program.

IVLP	International Visitor Leadership Program.
JBANC	Joint Baltic American National Committee.
JDL	Jewish Defense League.
KGB	Committee for State Security.
MAAG	Military Assistance Advisory Group.
MPAA	Motion Picture Association of America.
MXAT	Moscow Art Theater.
NATO	North Atlantic Treaty Organization.
NED	National Endowment for Democracy.
NGO	Non-Governmental Organization.
NIACT	Night Action.
OMGUS	Office of Military Government, US.
OWI	Office of War Information.
PPS	Polish Socialist Party.
PZPR	Polish United Workers Party.
RL	Radio Liberty.
SENO	South East North West.
SES	Soviet and East European Exchanges Staff.
SPLEX	Special Exchange.
SPO	Special Projects Office.
SUNY	State University of New York.
TASS	Telegraph Agency of the Soviet Union.
TIAS	Treaties and Other International Acts Series
UB	Polish Office of Security.
UCC	Universal Copyright Convention.
UPDK	Administration for Services to the Diplomatic Corps.
UPI	United Press International.
USAID	US Agency for International Development.
USIA	US Information Agency.
USICA	US International Communication Agency
USIS	US Information Service.
USOM	US Operations Mission.
VIP	Very Important Person.
VOA	Voice of America.

FOREWORD

Yale Richmond's memoir is timely. It comes when American prestige in the world is lower than it has been in recent memory, a shocking reversal of the situation when Mr. Richmond was working in the diplomatic trenches during the Cold War. The rising criticism of United States policy abroad, however, is not the result of the failure of public diplomacy—as some would have it—but of a failure of policy. Even the most vigorous public diplomacy cannot salvage a failed policy.

A few months before the United States invaded Iraq in 2003, former Speaker Newt Gingrich wrote an article calling for a purge of the professional staff of the State Department because, in his view, it showed insufficient zeal in carrying out the President's goal of spreading democracy in the world. Pointing to a leaked report from the State Department that said that democracy would not come instantly to Iraq if Saddam Hussein should be removed and therefore it would be necessary to insure public order from the start of any military occupation, Gingrich argued that this position contradicted President George W. Bush's statement that Iraqis were capable of democracy. It was, to him, a sign of disloyalty. Never mind that the State Department advice was accurate, and that the Administration's failure to heed it made much more difficult the goal of bringing democracy to Iraq. To Gingrich, and those of like mind, diplomacy, public or private, is simply propaganda, or—as they might put it—an advertising campaign for the president's policy.

This attitude brought to mind an incident a half century ago. Shortly after World War II, the Ford Motor Company announced the creation of a new automobile that was expected to take the nation by storm. Millions of dollars (back when they were worth at least ten of today's) were spent to publicize the new model. Speculation was intense, not only by automobile buffs, but among the public at large. I can well remember many conversations of neighbors wondering what this radically new car would really be like.

Finally, it was unveiled. What a let-down! It looked much like other medium-sized cars of the day, cost about the same, and had few, if any, features that would distinguish it from established models. Not many were sold; it was an even bigger bust than Coca-Cola's attempt, years later, to reformulate its popular drink.

I am sure that Ford executives who had been involved in planning the Edsel wished they could blame its failure on the advertising agency or the salesmen in dealerships. But that wouldn't wash. It was plain to all that Ford management had failed to build a car the public wanted. No amount of clever advertising or energetic salesmanship could sell a product the public did not want to buy. Instead of trying to find scapegoats outside their Dearborn headquarters, Ford executives absorbed the lesson, studied the market more carefully, and went on to create innovative successes such as the Thunderbird.

Today, the problem of America's image in the world is not that our public diplomacy is weak; it is that many current actions, as the rest of the world views them, are simply not salable. Just as Ford needed a different product, America needs to change some key policies if it is to restore its standing in world opinion.

Yale Richmond's memoir reminds us that pressures to politicize and propagandize official information and cultural exchange policy are nothing new. Mr. Richmond faced them in dealing with Frank Shakespeare, the director of the U.S. Information Agency during the Nixon administration. What the proponents of a propaganda approach to public diplomacy miss is that it just doesn't work. Accurate information, even when it is unpleasant or unfavorable, is essential for credibility. During the Cold War, professionals like Yale Richmond resisted the demands to engage in misleading propaganda, and they were usually successful in doing so. The fact that they kept American public diplomacy on an effective track made a major contribution to bringing the Cold War to a peaceful, negotiated end.

Many hard-bitten "realist" policy makers consider cultural and educational exchanges as, at best, ornamental trappings of foreign policy, merely "feel-good" activities. Nevertheless, it became clear as the Cold War came to a rapid end in the late 1980s, such exchanges had a profound effect in building support for radical change in Communist-ruled states. Some of the participants in the early exchanges, such as Alexander Yakovlev, became leaders of reform in Gorbachev's Soviet Union.

Communication at senior levels of government and expanding contacts by ordinary citizens also acted to bread down distrust and suspicion that had fueled the arms race. The same can be said of the 1975 Helsinki accords, denounced by many on the anti-Communist right as a sell-out—as Richmond points out. Contrary to the critics, the commitments in the Helsinki agreement provided the basis, first for opposition movements in Communist states, and subsequently for actual changes in Soviet and Soviet satellite practices.

Yale Richmond has done us a service in recounting the practical challenges that arise in conducting effective public diplomacy. His experiences give clear examples of what works and what doesn't. American officials charged with conducting public diplomacy can learn much from Richmond's experience, and members of the public with an interest in foreign affairs can gain insight into a professional specialty of enduring importance to America's security and standing in the world.

Jack F. Matlock, Jr.,
U.S. Ambassador to the Soviet Union, 1987-1991

PREFACE

Daddy, what do you do at the office? That question was often posed by my children for whom my work as a cultural officer presented puzzles. They had spent much of their childhood abroad, in Warsaw, Vienna, and Moscow, witnessing many of the events that were a part of my work. And in Washington, on Saturday mornings, they often accompanied me to the State Department where I sifted through piles of papers from American embassies in Moscow and other East European capitals.

Despite my explanations, my work remained a mystery to my children, as it does to most Americans who have never heard of the day-to-day work performed by their emissaries abroad, practicing Public Diplomacy in the winning of the Cold War. Or, more recently, seeking to repair the American image in countries around the world. Hence, this book.

What is Public Diplomacy? A term first coined in 1965 by Dean Edmund A. Gullion of Tufts University's Fletcher School of Law and Diplomacy:

> Public Diplomacy deals with the influence of public attitudes on the formation and execution of foreign policies. It encompasses dimensions of international relations beyond traditional diplomacy; the cultivation by governments of public opinion in other countries; the interaction of private groups and interests in one country with those of another; the reporting of foreign affairs and its impact on policy; communication between those whose job is communication, as between diplomats and foreign correspondents; and the processes of intercultural communications. Central to public diplomacy is the transnational flow of information and ideas.[1]

---

[1] http://fletcher.tufts.edu/murrow/public-diplomacy.html

INTRODUCTION

"Culture vulture" was the condescending term given to cultural officers by information officers of the United States Information Agency (USIA), the government agency charged with "Telling America's Story to the World," as its motto described its mission before it was merged into the State Department in 1999. Information officers were regarded as the elite of the agency, the glamour boys, and occasionally girls, who hobnobbed abroad with newspaper editors and foreign correspondents, and churned out press releases, pamphlets, and propaganda. Cultural officers, by contrast, labored unsung, expediting cultural and educational exchanges, working with writers, and mixing with musicians. Information was seen as hard and vital to winning the cold war of ideas. Culture was soft, and mere window dressing designed to show that America also had a culture. Less charitably, some called our work "Artsy fartsy."

But as the following pages will show, culture was a major factor in winning the hearts and minds of foreign audiences, and eventually the Cold War. Attending an American musical performance, seeing an American exhibit, hearing a lecture by a visiting American, borrowing a book from an American library, or better still, traveling to the United States on an exchange and seeing for themselves, turned out to be far more effective in winning those hearts and minds.

My years abroad practicing Public Diplomacy were in five countries of the Cold War—Germany, Laos, Austria, Poland, and the Soviet Union—each with new challenges and different from the other. Presenting a different kind of challenge was

Washington D.C., another Cold War hot spot at the center of Western power where I worked for eleven years at the State Department and three at USIA.

Germany, where I spent seven years (1947–1954), was where the Cold War began in the late 1940s, and where the US government initiated its "Reorientation Program," designed to bring democracy to Germans, and Germany back into the family of European nations. It was the first US effort in Public Diplomacy, talking directly to the people of a country rather than, as in traditional diplomacy, to their government or through their diplomats.

Next came two years (1954–1956) of Public Diplomacy in Laos, a country created after the French withdrawal from Indochina. It was two years of "nation building"—although the term had not yet been invented, or criticized—talking directly with the Lao people and helping to build and support a sense of nation in a country whose people did not know that they had a country.

That was followed by a year of Polish studies at Columbia University (1956–1957) in preparation for an assignment in Warsaw, and a year at the Voice of America (1957–1958) as director of broadcasts to Vietnam, talking to an audience of many millions in South and North Vietnam while waiting for a position to open for me in Warsaw. And then, three years (1958–1961) as cultural attaché in Poland, a Soviet "captive nation" that was open to reestablishing its historic cultural ties with the West.

In Vienna, Austria (1961–1963), I donned my information cap and worked with Western correspondents stationed there to report on Eastern Europe and the Soviet Union, helping to keep them, and their readers back home, informed about developments in those countries. That was followed by three years at the State Department in Washington (1963–1966), encouraging and facilitating exchanges of people between the US and Eastern Europe.

Next, after a year of Russian language study (1967–1967) at the Foreign Service Institute (FSI), I had my mission to Moscow (1967–1969). As the American Embassy's Counselor for Press and Culture, I worked on the Moscow end of US-Soviet exchanges, a vital part of Public Diplomacy, and learned how effective they could be in bringing about change in a country that had isolated itself from the West for so many years.

In all those foreign postings there was little guidance from Washington. We did receive a daily, unclassified "Wireless File," transmitted electronically from Washington (now called The Washington File), which provided a summary of news, especially bearing on our region of the world; full texts of US policy statements; and reports of speeches by leading US officials; all of which served as policy guidance for US diplomatic missions.[1] But beyond such general guidance, there was little direction from Washington on what we should be doing in Public Diplomacy at our posts abroad. For such guidance we depended on the "Country Team," composed of our chiefs of mission and their staffs.[2]

The remainder of my Foreign Service career (1969–1979) was served in Washington, working on a broad range of cultural and scientific exchanges with the Soviet Union and the countries of Eastern Europe.

After retiring from the Foreign Service in 1979, my cavalcade of Cold War activities continued with three years (1980–1983) at the Commission on Security and Cooperation in Europe (US Congress), monitoring implementation of the human rights and other provisions of the Helsinki Accords, and eight years (1983–1991) at the National Endowment for Democracy, encouraging democracy in the Soviet Union and Eastern Europe.

In all those years I was involved with the practice of Public Diplomacy and the making of history, with never a dull moment, but with many pleasant diversions with interesting people. In Moscow, as Embassy press spokesman, my pronouncements often turned up on US television where they were heard by President Lyndon B. Johnson, who had three televisions in his White House office tuned to the major networks. With that audience, mistakes were not permitted.

Less challenging duties brought after-hours pleasures. In Moscow, I danced with Gloria Swanson and had cocktails with Agnes de Mille and Sol Hurok. In Warsaw, I hosted visits by Mary McCarthy and Saul Bellow. And in Washington, I worked with

---

[1] For more on the Wireless File, see Wilson P. Dizard, Jr., *Inventing Public Diplomacy: The Story of the U.S. Information Agency* (Boulder: Lynne Rienner Publishers, 2004), 158–60.

[2] In later years there was also a Country Plan, outlining what we planned to do during the coming year, prepared at each USIS post and critiqued by USIA in Washington.

Norman Cousins, editor of *The Saturday Review of Literature*, to establish a series of meetings between American and Soviet writers.

Over those years I served seven administrations, Democrat and Republican, in five foreign countries. But it was in the Soviet Union and Poland, two countries with communist governments, where Public Diplomacy made the greatest contribution to US national interests. Hopefully, this book will help future US administrations to better appreciate its importance, and accord Public Diplomacy the recognition, and the funding, it deserves in other parts of the world.

Chapter 1

DOING DEMOCRACY IN DEUTSCHLAND

Germany was where the Cold War began, divided as it was into four zones of occupation—US, British, and French in the west; and Soviet in the east. It was where I began my forty-three-year career in the trenches of the Cold War. And it was where the United States first put Public Diplomacy into practice, although the term had not yet been thought up.

I arrived in Berlin in August 1947 as a US Military Government Intern, one of 100 young college graduates recruited to be the nucleus of a second generation of military governors in an occupation of Germany that was initially projected to last many years. A younger civilian component was thought necessary to complement, and eventually replace, the US Army officers who had stayed on to govern Germany after the hostilities of World War II had ended.

In June of that year I had received an electrical engineering degree, magna cum laude, from Syracuse University, and three good job offers, one of them a two-year training program at General Electric that would have made me a real engineer. But I was restless and not yet ready to settle down. Although I had served three years in the army during the war, I had not been overseas and felt that I had missed something. So, when I saw a notice on a bulletin board that the War Department—as a predecessor of the Defense Department was then known—was looking for 100 young men and woman to serve two years in Germany with the Office of Military Government, US (OMGUS), I promptly applied, was accepted, set my slide rule aside, and began what eventually became a career in international affairs with service in five countries that were hot spots in the Cold War.[1]

Berlin, a Western enclave within the Soviet Zone of Germany, was a bombed-out ruin when I arrived, a wrecked remnant of its powerful, imperial past. But it was the seat of the Allied Control Council (ACC), the four-power body composed of commanders-in-chief of the military forces of the occupying powers that were governing Germany. Governing the city of Berlin was another four-power military body, the *Komandatura,* a made-up word of Russian origin.

The two four-power bodies were still functioning in summer 1947, although from meetings of the Komandatura that I attended it was apparent that there was a deep rift between the Soviet Union and the three Western Powers. And only seven months later Marshal Vassily D. Sokolovsky and his Soviet delegation would walk out of an ACC meeting due to East-West differences, thus ending de facto four-power control of Germany and hastening the onset of the Cold War.

The glory of the formerly proud and lively capital of Germany was difficult to discern in 1947. Berliners were disillusioned, dispirited, and preoccupied mainly with a struggle for survival on the food they could scrounge in addition to the meager calories their ration cards provided. But there was as yet no wall dividing the city, and it was possible to take a subway train from West to East Berlin on the city's metrorail system. Streets had been cleared of rubble, but most of the vehicles on them were US Army Jeeps whose German drivers would gladly pick up passengers and take them anywhere in the city for an American cigarette or two, the informal currency.

Gen. Lucius D. Clay had succeeded Gen. Dwight D. Eisenhower as Military Governor of the US Zone of Germany on 15 March 1947. A career military officer and engineer, Clay came to office with a reputation for solving difficult problems, and there were plenty of them in Germany. As Military Governor he was responsible for food, housing, health, finances, industry, restoring wartime plunder, refugees, and denazification. Fair

---

[1] My appointment was as P-1, the lowest ranking professional class in those years, with an annual salary of $2,600. That was supplemented, however, by a 25 percent "hardship post" allowance for Germany and free housing. Other perks included access to the Army Post Exchange and officer clubs, tax-free German beer and other alcoholic drinks, free medical and dental care, and gasoline at 10 cents a gallon. The "hardship" was difficult to discern.

as well as firm, Berliners fondly called Clay *Pater Urbis* (City Father). He is also known as the father of the Berlin Airlift that sustained the city with food and other vital supplies during the Soviet blockade. Today a street in Berlin is named after him.[2]

After a month of familiarization in Berlin with the work of OMGUS, I was bound for Bavaria, a southern state in the US Zone. In dividing up Germany among the three western powers, it was said that the British got the industry, the French the wine, and the Americans the scenery. But in Bavaria I got some of each.

Munich, the capital of Bavaria at the foothills of the Alps, was a center of art, music, and industry, as well as the birthplace of the Nazi movement. But in 1947 it was merely another bombed-out remnant of a city, with skeletal ruins and piles of rubble everywhere. As elsewhere in Germany at the time, the impediments to recovery were staggering.

The German economy had collapsed, the government was gone, and the currency nearly worthless. A severe shortage of housing was aggravated not only by destroyed buildings but by a huge influx of Displaced Persons and twelve million German refugees who, in a modern-day ethnic cleansing, had been expelled or had fled from Eastern Europe, the Baltic states, and Russia where they had lived for centuries. Most of the German refugees and Displaced Persons were housed temporarily in camps in the US Zone, many of them in Bavaria, concentrated in and around Munich. Nevertheless, despite its many problems, Munich was slowly returning to life. Concerts were held and operas performed, but because the halls were not heated, winter audiences had to wear overcoats and hats in the concert halls. Life was grim but the remarkable German recovery was about to begin.

On 3 April 1948, President Harry Truman signed into law the European Recovery Program, commonly known as the Marshall Plan, which provided billions of dollars in material aid and technical assistance to European countries to aid in their economic recovery. And on 21 June, the Allies instituted a currency reform in the three western zones of Germany. The nearly worthless *Reichsmark* was replaced by the *Deutsche Mark,* which was initially pegged at 4.20 to a US dollar. Pessi-

---

[2] Here, I have drawn from James Dobbins et al., *America's Role in Nation-Building: From Germany to Iraq* (Santa Monica, CA: Rand Corporation, 2003), chapter 2.

mists predicted that the new mark would soon be useless—in Zürich it was selling for 20 to a dollar. But optimists traveled to Switzerland, purchased the new marks, and put them into Swiss accounts where they soon appreciated several fold. The Western effort to rebuild West Germany and integrate it into a democratic Europe had begun.

But on 24 June, two days after the Western commandants announced that they would introduce the new currency in West Berlin, the Soviets began their blockade of Berlin, cutting it off from the West, and two days later the Western Allies began their airlift to sustain the city. The Cold War heated up and Germany, as well as Berlin, was to remain divided for the next forty-two years.

In Munich I became familiar with the work of military government at the state level, and in the city of Rosenheim, at the city and county level. And it was in Bavaria that I learned to speak German, although with a Bavarian accent that I still have today.

Next came an assignment as executive officer of a military government detachment headquartered in Freising, a small town just northeast of Munich. There I performed administrative backstopping for military government officers in five counties, filled in for them when they were away on leave, and ran a motor pool with three German mechanics and some twenty cars, mostly big prewar Mercedes requisitioned from high Nazi officials, and a few Volkswagen "Beetles" newly off the postwar assembly line. I soon learned the names of all car parts in German, even before I knew them in English.

Military Government Officer

After a year of internship, I was appointed Military Government Officer for Wasserburg am Inn, a picturesque walled town on the Inn River, thirty miles east of Munich, whose streets and buildings, and some said mentality, had changed little since the Middle Ages.

In the months immediately after the war, the first military governors were in charge of local government. They appointed German officials and supervised their doings. But by the time I arrived in Wasserburg, elections had been held and local government had been turned over to the Germans. My authority, strictly speaking, was limited to foreign nationals and Displaced Persons, over whom the German authorities had no jurisdiction. However, it was only three years since the end of hostilities, and the United States was still an occupying power. The Germans addressed me as *Herr Gouverneur,* and deferred to me on many matters. The Soviet threat was not apparent in Wasserburg, but it was obvious that Germans preferred to be occupied by Americans rather than Russians.

One question bothered me as I departed for my first post where I would be completely on my own. How would Germans react to me as a Jew, and how would they explain the disappearance of a people who had lived in their midst for so many centuries? Who had been a Nazi, and who had not, and did it make a difference?[3]

Over the seven years that I spent in Germany I never encountered any overt manifestations of anti-Semitism. To be sure, Germans did not want to talk about what had befallen their Jewish neighbors but, I often wondered, did they know? Some undoubtedly knew, especially those who had served in the East in military or civilian capacities. But the vast majority, I came to believe, did not know because they were indifferent and did not want to know. Their Jewish compatriots had been "resettled" in the East, as the official Nazi explanation put it, and that explanation sufficed until incontrovertible evidence of the Holocaust later emerged.

My offices in Wasserburg were on the first floor of a small hotel overlooking the Inn River as it flowed around three sides of the town. My German staff consisted of three office employees, two drivers, a film projectionist, and a housekeeper for the three-bedroom house where I lived. And there, at the tender age of twenty-five I had legal jurisdiction over foreign nationals including a large camp of Displaced Persons, mostly Jewish refugees and survivors from Eastern Europe who were awaiting emigration to other countries.

In Wasserburg, I represented the United States in both town and county. The town was small, with a population of only some 6,000, but the county had another 54,000, many of them

---

[3] In the German national elections of 1928, the Nazi party finished ninth, with only 2.8 percent of the popular vote. But in 1932, in the last free election before the Nazis came to power, although still not winning a majority of the vote, the Nazi party placed first, with 37.2 percent.

wartime refugees from bombed-out German cities. Although I was the only American in the entire county and completely on my own, I felt perfectly safe and never had to carry a weapon.

It was in Wasserburg that I became a participant in the OMGUS Reorientation Program, as it was called, the first Public Diplomacy effort of the US government. The objective was to reorient the Germans to democracy by communicating directly with the people. "Reorientation" was chosen over "democratization" because the Russians, in their zone of Germany, had so abused the word democracy; and "reeducation" was rejected because it sounded too patronizing.

At war's end, German newspapers and radio stations had been established, directed, and staffed first by American military personnel, and then by Germans appointed by OMGUS. In major cities of the US Zone, American cultural centers, "America Houses," were opened with a variety of cultural and information programs for the German people.

At the local level, however, the Reorientation Program consisted mainly of encouraging the Germans to hold *Bürgerversammlungen* (town meetings), an innovation that was revolutionary for Germany and not without some controversy. The purpose was to encourage German citizens to question their elected officials on local issues and make the officials more responsive to the citizenry. Critics of the meetings, however, charged that they would reduce the authority of the newly elected officials who were either non-Nazis or had been cleared by denazification tribunals.

Nevertheless, with US encouragement the meetings were held, and German citizens, for the first time ever, were able to question their local officials in public forums. The meetings also had the support of owners of the inns where they were held, and where barrels of the good Bavarian beer were rolled out to be quaffed by the thirsty *Bürgers* and *Bauern* (townspeople and peasants) as they voiced their many complaints to their elected officials, and also to me as the representative of the occupying power.

Documentary film showings was another Public Diplomacy activity on the local level. As noted above, I had a film projectionist on my staff who toured the county in a Jeep with a 16 mm Bell & Howell projector, showing US documentary films dubbed with German sound tracks. The films, mostly on American and European themes, were intended to inform Germans about the United States, encourage democracy, and publicize the US role in European recovery through the Marshall Plan. Among the titles that I recall were *A Tuesday in November,* which described the US election process, and *Border Without Bayonets,* on how the United States and Canada lived peacefully side by side with a largely open border. The Marshall Plan films served to disseminate information about the European Recovery Program, provide technical assistance, and encourage economic cooperation among European nations. Other favorite films, although more for entertainment, were *Nanook of the North,* Robert Flaherty's epic of the Eskimo struggle to survive in the harsh, arctic environment, and Pare Lorentz's classics *The River* and *The Plow that Broke the Plains.* Because the Germans had been cut off from foreign media since 1939, the film showings proved very popular, and since they were shown in local *Gasthäuser* (inns), beer could be purchased during the showings.

It was in Wasserburg that I became a hunter. Farmers' fields were being devastated by deer that were multiplying unchecked. Because the Germans at that time were prohibited from possessing firearms, I was a frequent guest at organized hunts, provided I brought the guns and ammo.

Hunting in Europe is a sport of the well-to-do, and much different from the American sport. Hunters must rent a tract of land, called a *Revier* in German, which comes with exclusive hunting rights. They also hire a *Jagdmeister* (hunting master) who maintains the property, makes a count of the deer or elk, and determines how many have to be "harvested" each year to keep their numbers in check and keep the deer from devouring farm crops. Hunting often consists of sitting patiently in a stand as evening approaches, and waiting for the deer to come out and graze. The deer do not have much of a chance, and to Americans it does not seem like sport, but Germans can become avid hunters, as did many Americans who had guns. But for me it was a way to meet many important people in my public diplomacy efforts.

Resident Officer

As the Cold War continued with no hope of early resolution, the Federal Republic of Germany (FRG) was established by the three Western powers in September 1949, with its capital in Bonn, a small university town on the Rhine River, chosen because everyone knew it would be only the temporary seat of the new German government. In the FRG's first country-wide elections, the conservatives won, and Konrad Adenauer became chancellor (prime minister). US military government was replaced by a U.S. High Commission for Germany (HICOG), headed initially by John J. McCloy, a New York banker and former assistant secretary of war, and from 1953 to 1957 by James Bryant Conant, a renowned chemist and former Harvard University president. Ultimate authority, however, remained with the three Western occupying powers. My office in Wasserburg was closed, and I was assigned as Kreis (county) Resident Officer in Dinkelsbühl, a small town in central Bavaria, with responsibility for the three counties of Dinkelsbühl, Feuchtwangen, and Gunzenhausen, and a total population of 118,000.

The Resident Officer has been described as "the HICOG ambassador in the field and the jack-of-all-trades in the local administration of the occupation of Germany."[4] As McCloy described them, they were "probably the most important element in our relations with the German population."[5] In the US Zone, there were 157 such Resident Officers, serving as US representatives in cities and counties. Many were young Foreign Service Officers on their first assignment who later went on to successful careers as diplomats.

"Resident" had been the term used by the British for their colonial officers, and it was adopted by the Americans although the Germans were now mostly running the government, and the occupiers were no longer fully in charge, at least in the three Western zones. In Bavaria, however, the Germans called us *Residenz Offizier,* which must have sounded strange because a *Residenz* in German is the seat of a court or capital, and *Offizier* is a military officer.

The term Public Diplomacy had not yet been coined, but Resident Officers were tasked with encouraging support for Germany's transition to democracy and its reentry into a Europe that was making a start in the long process of unification. The

---

[4] *Kreis Resident Officer: Classification Standards Report,* Office of the U.S. High Commissioner for Germany (Bad Godesberg, Germany: July 1950), 1.

[5] Robert Shaplen, "Democracy's Best Salesmen in Germany," *Colliers* (9 February 1952), 27.

first step was the creation, in 1952, of the European Coal and Steel Community, which formed a common steel and coal market with freely set market prices and without import/export duties or subsidies. The economic aim was a common program of production and consumption of coal and steel, formerly the tools of war. The political objective was to demonstrate cooperation and reconciliation between France and Germany in the aftermath of the war, and a first step in the formation of a European union. The move had the strong support of the United States, and Resident Officers were tasked with selling it to the Germans at the grassroots level, which we did with our films and public speaking.

In our cities and counties Resident Officers were the eyes and ears of the US government, and often the mouth as well. In public meetings I was often called upon to explain, in my by that time fluent German, the reforms the United States was urging the new German government to adopt. Among them were: in economics, to establish freedom of trade to end the closed guild system, encourage economic growth, and provide business opportunities for German refugees from the East; in education reform, to end the two-track system in public schools and open higher education to everyone;[6] and in agriculture, to end "strip farming" and consolidate the inherited small strips of land into more efficient units of farmland.

Also requiring my attention at times was a US signals intelligence unit, stationed on a hill at the edge of Dinkelsbühl town from where it monitored radio broadcasts from the East.

The OMGUS Reorientation Program was transferred to HICOG. Its objectives, as stated in the bureaucratese and cold war rhetoric of the time, were:

1) to strengthen in the German people the will for and knowledge of democratic self-government and repugnance for authoritarian rule, whether from the left or the right;

2) to contain and counter the propaganda of Communists and extreme nationalists hostile to democracy and to Allied and United States purposes in Germany;

---

[6] Under the two-track system, Germans had to decide, at an early age, whether to attend schools that prepared them for worker or clerical jobs, or schools that led to universities and higher education study.

3) to explain and to gain acceptance and support of United States policy, especially as it concerns the political integration of Germany into Western Europe and the economic objectives of the European Recovery Program;

4) to promote better understanding and friendship between the United States and a reconstituted Germany.[7]

The Reorientation Program was extensive and expensive. At its peak in 1952, its annual budget for the former US Zone was close to $48 million, and the HICOG staff in that year numbered 7,046, of whom 594 were Americans, a larger US representation than in any other country.[8] As Henry J. Kellerman, director of the Office of Public Affairs in the State Department, noted, "A most useful element in implementing this multidimensional character of this program proved to be the use of the Kreis Resident Officers who helped extend its benefits to the grassroots level."[9]

Resident Officers were urged not to be desk bound. As Charles W. Thayer, US Consul General in Munich, advised us, "Get out to towns and villages, buy *Bürgermeisters* a beer and talk with them about the United States and what we are trying to do here."[10] It was Public Diplomacy at the grassroots level: as we talked with mayors about US policy, promoted reforms in Germany, attended the town meetings we encouraged the Germans to hold, and showed the flag in a Germany we had been at war with only five years earlier.

---

[7] Henry J. Kellerman, *Cultural Relations as an Instrument of US Foreign Policy: The Educational Exchange Program Between the United States and Germany 1945–1954*, Department of State Publication 8931, International Information and Cultural Series 114, March 1978, 83.

[8] Ibid., 89.

[9] Ibid., 85.

[10] Charles W. Thayer, a West Point graduate, had parachuted into Yugoslavia during World War II where he served as a US liaison officer to Tito and his partisans. After the war, he joined the Foreign Service, served in Moscow, and authored two hilarious books about his adventures and escapades. The quote is from a meeting in Nuremberg the author attended. Fifty-five years later Colin Powell, another solider turned diplomat, in an address at the State Department on Foreign Affairs Day 2004, advised an audience of Foreign Service retirees to get out and talk to people about what the United States was doing in the world.

Those duties of the Resident Officer sound today remarkably similar to the new US policy of Transformational Diplomacy announced by Secretary of State Condoleeza Rice, on 18 January 2006. Its purpose, said Rice, is "to work with our many partners around the world to build and sustain democratic, well-governed states that will respond to the needs of their people—and conduct themselves responsibly in the international system" and "to take America's story directly to the people."[11]

Future Resident Officer assignments took me to Pfaffenhofen an der Ilm and Schweinfurt, where I had further opportunities to take America's story directly to the people.[12]

Pfaffenhofen was the headquarters of the signals intelligence unit that I was familiar with from Dinkelsbühl, and the site of a Displaced Persons camp of Kalmyks, a Buddhist people from the steppes of Russia between the Don and Volga Rivers who had fled from Stalinist oppression.[13] Otherwise, there would have been no need to have a US diplomatic presence in Pfaffenhofen. The county was small, with no industry. Its main product was hops, a vital ingredient of the good Bavarian beer. And thanks to the hops crop, we had a culinary treat each spring when local restaurants served the delicious Hopfenspargel (asparagus hops), the blossom of the hops vine.

One of the more interesting characters in Pfaffenhofen was a former mayor, Josef Rath, a cook by profession, who had been appointed by the American military as the first postwar Bürgermeister because he spoke English and had not been a Nazi party member. Before the war Rath had been a cook at the elite Hotel Kempinski in Berlin, and had learned his English in the United States during the 1930s when he cooked at New York's Waldorf Astoria and at Florida hotels during the winters. In retirement, Rath kept his culinary arts well honed by the occasional dinners he prepared for me in the rudimentary kitchen of his modest home. And I learned a lot from him about local politics in Pfaffenhofen.

---

[11] US Department of State Fact Sheet, Office of the Spokesman, 18 January 2006.

[12] Resident Officers were often moved after a year in place, partly because of reorganizations but also because some higher-ups did not want us to get too close to the Germans.

[13] The Kalmyks are the only Buddhist people in Europe.

Schweinfurt

Increased responsibilities and promotion quickly followed, and next came a more interesting assignment as Resident Officer in Schweinfurt, an industrial city on the Main River in Franconia, northern Bavaria, with a population of some 48,000 in the city and another 56,000 in the county. As the ball bearing manufacturing center of Germany, the city had been heavily bombed by the US Army Air Forces during the war, and although only factories had been targeted, damage to the center of the city was severe. Over half the houses had been left uninhabitable, but recovery was well under way when I arrived in August 1950. The inner city had been rebuilt, and the factories were again humming.

Schweinfurt had been a free imperial city from 1282 to 1803, and it consequently had a long tradition of independence in politics. Its most famous son was the poet Friedrich Rückert, born there in 1788 and whose statue stands in the town square across from the beautiful Renaissance *Rathaus* (town hall), built in 1572. And in that Rathaus, visitors will find the Golden Book of the city, in which signatures of prominent visitors have been inscribed over the years. My signature is there for 1950, but a few years back visitors will also find the signatures of Heinrich Himmler, head of Hitler's SS, and other high-ranking Nazis.

The city, however, had not been a Nazi stronghold because its blue-collar electorate generally voted Socialist or Communist. When I arrived all the major political parties were represented and national politics were replicated on the local level. The major parties included the left-of-center Social Democrat, the conservative Christian Social, the liberal (in the European sense) Free Democrat, and the far-left Communist. The city had heavy industry, was historically Protestant, and voted Social Democrat; the county was agricultural, conservative, Catholic, and voted Christian Social. But many of Schweinfurt's industrial workers were also farmers. They pedaled to their workplaces in the city on their bikes in the morning, and returned home in the evening to work their farms. Schweinfurt was a great introduction to European politics, and I learned there more than I ever could have from textbooks. I took advantage of every opportunity to speak at public events—political party meetings, high school graduations, and "roof raisings" at new housing projects funded by the Marshall Plan. Those events provided experience in Public Diplomacy that I would put to good use in future Foreign Service assignments.

It was in Schweinfurt that I attended my first, and only, Communist Party meeting. The local party organization would hold frequent public meetings to organize protests against US policy in Germany. To keep myself informed, I decided to attend one such meeting, called to protest against the *Kartoffelkäfer* (potato beetle), which the communists alleged had been spread by Americans in the Soviet Zone where it was devouring the potato crop.

The Schweinfurt communist leaders were on the dais, and they recognized me in the audience. When they called for a vote in support of a resolution condemning the *Amikäfer*, the term they used for the "American" potato beetle, everyone in the hall raised his hand except me. When they next asked for votes opposed to the resolution, no one raised a hand, including me. And then, in an obvious attempt to embarrass me, the party chairman announced he would have to assume that everyone in the hall supported the resolution. Fortunately for me the incident was not reported in the local press, and I was spared embarrassment. But I had learned a lesson—to be cautious about attending political meetings.

The Soviet threat was more evident in Schweinfurt than in my previous assignments. Soviet aggressive intentions in Europe may have been exaggerated at the time, but the Korean War had just started, and for the US military in Germany the Soviet threat was real. US forces in Germany had been largely demobilized after the war, and all that remained was the equivalent of two divisions. Facing them on the other side of a divided Germany were twenty-five forward-deployed Soviet divisions, backed up by many more divisions and aircraft based in the Soviet Union, only a few hundred miles to the east. And when communist North Korea invaded South Korea in June 1950, who could blame the West for fearing a Soviet invasion of Western Europe, starting in occupied Germany? Military plans are based on the capabilities of adversaries, not their intentions. In the immediate postwar years, the main mission of US forces in Germany had been occupation and control, but by 1950, in response to Soviet military deployments, that mission had changed to the defense of Western Europe.

Stationed in Schweinfurt was a squadron of the US Constabulary, a lightly-armed mechanized-cavalry unit, equivalent to a battalion but equipped only with Jeeps and armored cars. Its mission was to patrol and show the flag along Bavaria's border with the Soviet Zone of Germany, a mere twenty miles to the northeast as the crow flies. But when a general from the US European Command visited Schweinfurt after the Korean War had broken out and learned how long it would take the squadron to get to the border, he ordered a unit to immediately take up a position closer to the border, where they could act as a tripwire for invading Soviet forces.

Germany and Korea had both been divided in the aftermath of World War II, and West German fears over a possible invasion from the East were understandable. To reassure the Germans, the United States increased its military forces in Germany and staged a flight of B-29 bombers ~~~~~~~~~ in Britain. I happened to be in Munich at th~~ the big bombers, which had not been seen i~~ World War II, passed over at low altitude, th~~ very reassuring to the Germans. And that t~~ Public Diplomacy.

Civil affairs—relations between the US ~~ Schweinfurt authorities—was one of my res~~ tunately, incidents were few and limited mo~~ ~~~~~~~~~~~ cidents, traffic violations, drunks, and other minor incidents. But there was one event that was more serious and involved the Schweinfurt *Oberbürgermeister* (mayor). Our Constabulary squadron was scheduled to play a football game with another US military team, and the city administration had given its permission to use the Schweinfurt municipal stadium. As a courtesy the mayor was invited to attend the game. The mayor thought he would be attending a *Fussball* (soccer) game, and was appalled when he witnessed his beautiful soccer field being torn up by rampaging American football players. It took a lot of turf mending before cordial relations with the mayor were restored.

As Resident Officer I also had to deal with the big split in German politics between the two major political parties, the left-of-center Social Democrat and the right-of-center Christian Democrat (Christian Social in Bavaria). The Social Democrats, under the leadership of Kurt Schumacher, supported us on German domestic reform but generally opposed us on foreign policy. The Christian Democrats, led by Chancellor Konrad Adenauer, supported us on foreign policy but opposed many of our domestic reforms. It required some fancy footwork to stay on good terms with both parties at the local level.

All was not work in Schweinfurt, and one of its attractions was the wine. The city is located in a large wine-growing region along the Main River, and it was there that I acquired a taste for the *Franken* (Franconia) wines in their distinctive green *Bocksbeutel* bottles. As the Franconians told me, their wine is not exported because so much of it is consumed at home that there is little left to export. During my time in Schweinfurt, I helped to validate that claim.

I entertained often in my big house on the Kiliansberg, so named after the Irish bishop who brought Christianity to Franconia in the seventh century. Over food and wine I made the acquaintance of many of the city's political and social activists, and practiced Public Diplomacy at the dining room table. When I invited the heads of the major Schweinfurt trade unions to dinner and a discussion of their concerns and mine, they told me that I was the first American to pay any attention to them.

Many friends were made in Schweinfurt, several of whom I would like to mention here. Chief Judge Carl Friedrich Wolfgang Behl (known in literary circles as C.F.W. Behl) was a distinguished writer and critic as well as jurist. He had been a lawyer in Berlin and secretary to the renowned German dramatist Gerhart Hauptmann, 1912 Nobel Laureate in Literature.[14]

Theo Brock, a physician with whom I talked politics on many an evening, was a local leader of the Free Democratic Party. Georg Schäfer was the head of Kugelfischer, the big family-owned ball and roller bearing plant. On a tour of the plant he once gave me, the paternalist Schäfer greeted many of his workers by their first names, and pointed out those whose fathers had also worked at the plant. And Oskar Serrand, Kugelfischer's financial director, and his charming wife Meta, who organized wild boar hunts to which I was invited—with my guns of course.

The only thing I left in Schweinfurt was an American reading room, which I opened at a ceremony attended by US Land Commissioner for Bavaria George N. Shuster and Oberbürgermeister Ignaz Schoen.[15] But I took with me much more—pleasant

---

[14] Behl's son, Wolfgang, emigrated to the United States where he became a distinguished sculptor.

[15] Shuster, a prominent Catholic layman, had been president of New York City's Hunter College.

memories, mementos from many well wishers, more experience in communicating with the public, and a good introduction to European politics.

Cultural Exchange

My final years in Germany, 1951–1954, were spent sequentially in Munich, Nuremberg, and Stuttgart, working on the "Exchange Program," as we called it, which sent thousands of Germans to the United States—high school and university students, teachers, professors and scholars, journalists, and political and trade union leaders. In one year alone, 1952, 3,415 Germans were participants in programs that brought them to the United States for visits of three months to one year.[16] Begun as a unilateral effort emphasizing German students and younger leaders, and financed solely by the United States, it eventually evolved into a binational Fulbright program in which the German financial contribution was larger than the American. Today there is hardly a leading figure in any branch of German life who has not participated in one of the US exchange programs. It was the most effective part of our public diplomacy effort in Germany. Seeing is believing.

As Exchanges Officer for Northern Bavaria stationed in Nuremberg, I had a free hand in selecting Germans for the Leader Program, as it was called then, which later became the State Department's International Visitor Program (IVP), and more recently, the International Visitor Leadership Program (IVLP).[17] American ambassadors have consistently rated the Leader Program, whatever it is called, as the most important of all US exchange programs.

Based on my experience in Schweinfurt, I believed that preference should be given to Social Democrats, since they were in the opposition during the Adenauer years and needed to have a better understanding of the United States and its domestic and foreign policies. Accordingly, I tended to favor them in my nominations to Washington. That attracted the attention of administrators of the exchanges, since most of my

---

[16] Kellerman, *Cultural Relations*, 89.

[17] Each new US administration, when it continues a proven program of the previous administration, for some reason feels obliged to change its name.

colleagues in other parts of Germany were nominating people who were more supportive of American foreign policy. When I returned to Washington once on home leave, I was welcomed at the State Department with the greeting, "So you're the one who has been sending us all those socialists." I took that as a compliment, recognizing that one day the Social Democrats would form the government of Germany, which indeed happened when Willy Brandt became chancellor in 1969, and Helmut Schmidt in 1974.

The results of our German exchange program are readily apparent today, when we see a democratic Germany committed to a free market and the rule of law, a member of NATO and the European Union, and an integral part of Europe moving toward union. As Willy Brandt described the benefits of US-German exchanges:

> We must get to know each other better, still more: We must learn to live with each other. More young Europeans must have the opportunity of exploring the social landscape of America, of discovering America's outlook on life, of becoming familiar with its history, and the process must be reciprocal.[18]

I am pleased to have played a minor role in that Cold War victory. But for me personally, the experience of working on a broad and multi-faceted exchange program in Germany proved invaluable in later assignments in Warsaw and Moscow, where exchanges were also an important part of our public diplomacy efforts during the Cold War.

In July 1951, on the recommendation of a State Department Personnel Selection Panel, I was appointed to the Career Foreign Service after an interview in which I was queried on my knowledge of American history and German affairs, and tested on my German-language competence. But I suspect that the real reason for my favorable recommendation was that I had learned a lot while managing to stay out of trouble in a postwar Germany where the temptations for a young and single American were many. It's not that I was celibate, but I heeded what an older and more experienced American had advised me. "In the towns where you are assigned," he said, "the Germans will

---

[18] Quoted in Ulrich Littmann, "Perspectives from Bonn," in *International Educational and Cultural Exchange* (US Advisory Commission on International and Cultural Affairs, Department of State) 10, no. 2, (1974).

know what you had for breakfast, and with whom you had it. So, if you must have female companionship, make sure it is not in the town where you are resident."

After seven years in Germany, I received a real Foreign Service assignment in 1954. Due to my five years of high school and college French, bachelor status, and good health, I was assigned to Vientiane, the administrative capital of the newly independent Kingdom of Laos in the former French Indochina, where new challenges in Public Diplomacy awaited me.

Chapter 2

NATION BUILDING IN LAOS

When the French garrison at Dien Bien Phu fell to the communist-led Vietminh on 7 May 1954, it marked the end of ninety years of French colonial rule in Indochina. Two months later, the Geneva Accords called for a temporary division of Vietnam at the seventeenth parallel, to be followed by "free and fair elections" monitored by the international community. The sovereignty and territorial integrity of Laos and Cambodia, the two other parts of Indochina, were also recognized.

Little landlocked Laos became a constitutional monarchy with a king, Sisavang Vong, resident in the remote royal capital of Luang Prabang in the north, and a government and parliament in Vientiane, a sleepy little town in the central region. Pending a political settlement with the Royal Lao government, the pro-North Vietnamese Pathet Lao, who had fought with the Vietminh against the French, were allowed to regroup in the two northern provinces they already controlled. To monitor the provisions of the Geneva Accords, including a ceasefire, an International Control Commission, with members from Canada, India, and Poland, was established.

Laos itself had little real importance to the United States—then and now it was one of the poorest countries in Asia—but it was seen by Washington at the time as one of the "dominos" in Southeast Asia. According to the domino theory of US Secretary of State John Foster Dulles, if Laos or Cambodia fell to the communists, Thailand would be next, and that could eventually mean the loss of all Southeast Asia. And that is how little Laos, with a population of perhaps only two million in

1954—no one is really sure of the number—became a bone of contention between its communist, neutralist, and rightist factions, and another hot spot in the Cold War between the superpowers. And that is where Public Diplomacy became an important tool of US foreign policy.

I arrived in Laos in June 1954 one month after the fall of Dien Bien Phu. The US objective there was to support the Royal Lao government in its efforts to prevent an insurgent movement, the pro-communist Pathet Lao, from taking over the country. But most of the Lao people did not know that they lived in a sovereign state. Information about Laos and the rest of the world was sparse. The government operated a few low-power radio stations and published a daily information bulletin in Lao and French, based on the *Agence France Presse* (AFP) wire service, but illiteracy was high and the reach of the radio and print media did not extend beyond the few provincial capitals. Radio broadcasts from Thailand could be received, but the low-cost transistor radio had not yet come to Laos. The term "nation building" had not yet been coined and we had no example to follow, but over the next two years my colleague Ted Tanen and I accomplished a few major achievements in Public Diplomacy.

First, we began publication of a Lao-language edition of USIA's monthly photo magazine, *Free World,* featuring articles designed to strengthen the Royal Lao government's public image and provide information about the history, culture, and politics of Laos and the other countries of Southeast Asia, as well as US aid to Laos. The magazine was printed at USIA's big printing plant in Manila, but I took the photos and wrote the copy in English. Because there were few Laotians who knew English in those years, we had the articles translated first into Thai by a local Thai employee, and then from Thai to Lao by a Lao local. To check the translation, a third Lao employee translated it into French, which we could read. That apparently worked because we never had any complaints about language or content.

Next, we produced a monthly Lao-language newsreel highlighting news of the Lao government, the royal family, and US assistance to Laos. With 16 mm projection equipment that we gave to Lao province chiefs—the same Bell & Howell projectors that I had used in Germany—along with small gasoline-powered mobile generators, the newsreels, with a Lao-language sound track, were shown in villages where people had never seen a movie or even an electric light bulb. I had never produced a film, but until we were able to hire motion picture professionals from Manila and Saigon, I was camera man, script writer, and editor.

And third, we distributed large colorful posters with a photo of the Buddha and the Lao king, and distributed them throughout the provinces controlled by the Royal Lao government where they became a fixture on the walls of village homes.

Another means of disseminating information was to use the Mekong River, one of the great rivers of the world, as a medium of communication. The Mekong rises in the highlands of Tibet and wends its way some 3,000 miles through China, Myanmar (Burma), Thailand, Laos, Cambodia, and Vietnam before reaching the South China Sea. In Laos it is the main artery of the country, and along its banks and tributaries live most of the ethnic Lao people. To reach them we hired a boat and a team of Mohlam singers, the traditional "wandering minstrel" way of spreading the word in Laos. Our showboat cruised up and down the rivers, providing entertainment and information with film showings and songs of news to village people.

It was a tough, two-year, tropical tour. The skilled Vietnamese technicians and minor officials whom the French had brought with them to administer the government bureaucracy and maintain the public utilities had been driven or fled from Laos during the First Indochina War, and public services were almost nonexistent.[1] There was no running water, and electricity supply was intermittent. But we had more than our share of tropical diseases, limited medical care, and hazardous air travel. As Seymour "Max" Finger, later our deputy chief of mission put it, "There are only two kinds of Americans in Laos— those who have amoebic dysentry [*sic*], and those who don't know it.[2] I was in the latter category and didn't learn that I had amoebiasis until many years later.

As the amoeba in our guts multiplied, so did the staff of the US mission. During my two years in Laos the number of Americans grew from five to more than a hundred, but Ted Tanen

---

[1] The First Vietnam War, 1946–1954, fought by the French, ended with the battle of Dien Bien Phu.

[2] Seymour "Max" Finger, quoted in Oden Meeker, *The Little World of Laos* (New York: Charles Scribner's Sons, 1959), 214.

and I were the pioneers in Public Diplomacy. And we did it without any guidance from Washington, which was just as well because few in Washington knew anything about Laos.

The Mekong River separates Laos from Thailand but the river, longer than the Mississippi, provides only an artificial boundary. The Lao and Thai people are members of the same ethnic group, and their languages are mutually intelligible. Moreover, in Laos people on both banks of the Mekong are ethnic Lao, speak the same language, and are often related by marriage. However, Siam, as Thailand was formerly known, had been able to maintain its independence from the British encroaching from India and Burma on their west, and the French on their east, advancing into what used to be called Indochina. And until the French came up the Mekong River into Laos in the 1860s, the King of Siam considered much of Laos to be under his suzerainty.

The people of Laos are a collection of many ethnic groups and languages. The Thai-Lao, who constitute some 70 percent of the population and are sometimes known as Valley Lao, live along the Mekong River and its many tributaries, and are growers and consumers of rice. The aboriginal Mon-Khmer, some 20 percent of the population, are highland people who live in middle-altitude areas of northern and southern Laos. The Sino-Tibetans, about 10 percent, and the most recent arrivals, are hill people who have migrated from southern China, Tibet, and Myanmar into Laos and northern Vietnam over the past century. Moreover, each of the more than sixty minority tribes of Laos has its own culture, language, and way of life. Out of that melange of cultures and languages the French had created a new nation, *Le Laos,* by cobbling together the northern provinces centered around Luang Prabang, the southern provinces of Champassak, and the central provinces around Vientiane and Savannakhet. Buddhism was the predominant religion of the country, with animism common in the mountain regions.

Having just completed five years as a cultural officer in Germany, not a typical Foreign Service assignment, I was looking forward to a real Foreign Service posting. Little did I realize that Laos would be as atypical as Germany, but much more dangerous and far less comfortable.

Like many countries of Southeast Asia, Laos had some elements of a tropical paradise. The people were gentle, soft spoken, peaceful, and outwardly passive. They had a popular saying, *boh pen nyang,* roughly translated as "It doesn't matter" or "It's okay." The staples of their diet—rice, fish, vegetables, and fruit—were plentiful, except in rare years of drought. Public health, however, as in most developing countries at the time, was rudimentary at best. Longevity for adults was only in the early forties, and half of all newborns did not live beyond two years.

The administrative capital, Vientiane, despite its sub-equatorial climate and high humidity, had been a comfortable post in French colonial days. But it had been neglected by the French during the First Indochina War, and in 1954 it was a run-down town of perhaps 20,000, lacking dependable public services.

The American presence in Laos in 1954 was a holding action, awaiting a US decision on what to do about Vietnam, and it seemed that no one in Washington cared much about Laos or the American staff there. A legation had been opened in 1951, and when I arrived the mission was headed by Chargé d'affaires Lloyd "Mike" Rives, an FSO-6, the lowest rank in those years.[3] The staff also included Ted Kobrin, CIA Station Chief; Ted Tanen, Public Affairs Officer; and Nan MacKay, representing the US Operations Mission (USOM), a field unit of what is now the US Agency for International Development (USAID). I was Information Officer, and junior officer at the post.

With such a small staff, housing initially was not a problem. Nan MacKay had her own "bungalow," as the French called her little house, but the rest of us, four bachelors, shared a communal life in the chief-of-mission's residence, a comfortable French-style villa on the bank of the Mekong River. The chancery, where official business was conducted, was located in the residence and consisted of one room and an adjoining lavatory that doubled as code room.

In the evening, after a hot but not hard day's work, we gathered at the dinner table, dining on whatever our Vietnamese *bep (*cook) had managed to purchase that day. Much of what we ate came from across the Mekong River in Thailand. The meat, we surmised, was water buffalo, served almost daily. Each evening, as dessert was being served—usually a French flan—a messenger from the Lao Post Office would arrive by bicycle bearing the day's telegrams from Washington. Most of

---

[3] The State Department, in those years, maintained legations, rather than embassies, in smaller countries. The Vientiane legation was elevated to embassy in August 1955.

them were NIACT (Night Action), which had to be answered that night, and Mike Rives would retire to the code room to decode them by hand on the old "one-time pad" system.

A few days after my arrival, I was summoned to pay a courtesy call on Prime Minister Souvanna Phouma, one of the few real statesmen in Southeast Asia in those years. Donning my crisp white linen suit, I set out on foot for the prime minister's office and residence a few blocks away. After introductory pleasantries, Prince Souvanna asked if I had brought a message for him from Secretary Dulles. I disappointed him by replying that, unfortunately, Mr. Dulles had been unable to meet with me before my departure from Washington.

As low man on the American diplomatic totem pole in Laos, I had only a few direct dealings with Souvanna during my two-year tour of duty in Laos. But when Souvanna visited Poland in 1961, I was in the reception line at the Warsaw airport and, as the only familiar face, I was greeted by him with a big smile and a hearty handshake.

In summer 1954, Charles W. Yost, a veteran career Foreign Service Officer, arrived as minister and chief-of-mission. Yost was soon followed by a host of other officers—political, economic, and administrative—and military attachés, communication clerks, secretaries, Marine guards, and a large economic assistance mission. The one-room chancery became rather crowded—probably the first time a minister had to share an office with his entire staff—and a US Army field tent was set up in the residence garden as legation annex.

To that primitive post in February 1955 came Secretary of State John Foster Dulles, with a large entourage of officials and journalists. Among the many problems facing the new Lao government was its army, which provided security against the Vietminh and Pathet Lao but had not been paid for months. After the Dulles visit, Washington moved quickly to support the Lao government and give aid directly, rather than through the French. The first payment soon arrived—a $2 million check, the first of many that were to follow.

Yost wanted to make a formal presentation of the check to symbolize American support, and I went along to take photos. Our lone legation vehicle was a battered Jeep station wagon, which we drove ourselves since there was no legation driver. But the latch on the driver's door was broken, making it necessary to drive with the right hand and hold the door closed with the left. Yost pocketed the check and we piled into the Jeep, with the minister in the driver's seat. I thought it would look bad enough for the United States to be delivering two million dollars in an old Jeep, but even worse for the minister to be driving it, so Yost accepted my offer to drive. Thus, we arrived more or less in style for the presentation to Lao Premier Katay Don Sasorith, a pro-Thai Lao nationalist who had succeeded neutralist Souvanna Phouma.[4]

Another member of the Lao royal family I met was Crown Prince, and later King, Savang Vattana, a cousin of Souvanna Phouma. When Minister Yost made his introductory call on the crown prince in Luang Prabang in January 1955, I went along and took with me one of our 16 mm film projectors and a film to show after dinner in the royal palace. The crown prince had once expressed a desire to travel across the United States by Greyhound bus, and USIA obliged by sending us a Greyhound documentary film of such a journey. I had never before dined with royalty, and I still remember the delicious *cuissot de chevreuil rôti* (roasted haunch of venison), which we washed down with a Mouton Rothschild. The following day, on an excursion up the Mekong by pirogue, we saw the miniature Buddhas in the famed Pak Ou caves upstream from Luang Prabang, and had a *pique-nique* on a river sandbar on the return trip. The Lao are well known for their hospitality.

Back in Vientiane, funds became available to lease a chancery building and provide housing and support for the American staff, which was increasing day by day. Housing was the immediate need. Initially, we bachelors continued to share the residence with Yost, doubling and tripling up in the few bedrooms. But when Mrs. Yost arrived, the first American spouse in Vientiane, we had to find other quarters. The few French-built villas were occupied by Lao government ministers and other diplomatic missions, and what was left were mostly thatch and bamboo houses on stilts.

I moved into a temporary USIS office, formerly a shop just off the marketplace, and there I worked and slept for several weeks, although the nearest toilet was two blocks away in the legation. Eventually, the legation found two villas, one for single men, and the other for single women. Beds could not be purchased locally, so our Army attaché had canvas folding cots

---

[4] Katay, who succeeded Souvanna Phouma as premier, governed 1954–1956.

flown in. Because there were not enough cots to go around, our two Marine guards had to share one, which was not as unusual as it may sound since each worked a twelve-hour shift seven days a week.

The French-built villas were designed for the tropics, with thick masonry walls, high ceilings, tile floors, lots of open windows—no glass or screens, of course—but few basic conveniences. We slept under mosquito nets, sharing our bedrooms with ten-inch, alligator-like gecko lizards that would stare at us at night from walls on the other side of our nets. Laotians told us not to worry—geckos in the house are a sign of good luck.

Electricity was available only in the center of town and not where we lived, but the old generator, when it worked, provided 50-volt current for only a few hours in the evening. Our refrigerator burned kerosene and cooled very efficiently. Water was delivered by truck, dumped into an open cistern at the rear of the house, and pumped by hand to 55-gallon drums on the roof, which gave us a gravity feed for a shower and toilet. When there was no truck, which was quite often, there was no shower and no flush. Fortunately, the Mekong was only one block away. Eventually, a gasoline-powered US Army field generator arrived that gave us 110 volts but created an awful roar in our backyard. The water problem was never solved.

Vientiane in those years was a calm and peaceful post. The Lao people like to party, and our social life was active. We had no need for house guards, and slept with doors and windows wide open. It was a relatively safe post, except for the time when I was almost killed.

Shortly after my arrival I received two invitations for a Saturday night dinner. One was from Deputy Prime Minister Phoui Sananikone, who wanted to meet the new American diplomat in town. The other was from a French archaeologist named Charles Archambault, married to a beautiful princess of the Shan tribe of northeast Myanmar who are related to the Lao and speak a similar language. The Archambaults, visiting in Vientiane, were authorities on Laos, and very pertinent for me, so I accepted their invitation and "regretted" the one from Sananikone.

The Frenchman and his wife gave me a great introduction to Laos. But at the home of the deputy prime minister, as the guests were chatting after dinner, someone tossed two hand grenades through an open window and opened fire with a pistol, killing Minister of Defense Kou Voravong, a political rival of the host, and wounding several other guests. The assassination was never solved, but the first thing I did when I heard about it the next morning was to send a telegram to my mother saying I was okay, although I came very close to having my name on the plaque in the State Department lobby inscribed with names of Foreign Service personnel who have died in the line of duty.

Isolation was Vientiane's main hardship. The French had built a good road network, but much of it had been destroyed during the war or had deteriorated through lack of maintenance. The roads that remained were threatened by the communist-led Pathet Lao guerrillas and were impassible during the rainy season. Air was the only sure way to travel, but it was not always safe or dependable.

The legation was served by two flights a week from Saigon, via Phnom Penh, by Civil Air Transport, the airline started after World War II by US Gen. Claire L. Chennault of "Flying Tigers" fame. The pilots were American and Chinese who flew sturdy, dependable, and well-maintained DC-3 aircraft—known in its military version as the C-47—that could accommodate passengers as well as freight. What was not publicly known at the time [but which we all surmised] was that the CIA had purchased the airline, which later became known as Air America and would play a major role in America's secret war in Laos.

For flights within Laos, the local airline, Air Laos, provided service to the provinces, as well as to Phnom Penh and Saigon, flying DC-3s that the French called Dakotas. The pilots were French, very experienced, and knew the terrain well, and where to land in an emergency. Maintenance, however, was at best haphazard. The planes had bucket seats along the sides but no seat belts. When we took off, laden with passengers and freight, the passengers often had to stand forward, bunched up behind the bulkhead to move the center of gravity forward and give us better lift. Flying during the monsoon season could be even more scary as a plane might suddenly drop in altitude, and you wondered whether the wings were going to fall off. The landing strips were grass or perforated interlocking sections of metal that the US Seabees had used in World War II.

I vowed never to go on an inaugural flight after a close call with an Air Laos flight initiating new service to a province deep

in the mountains of northern Laos. It promised to be an interesting trip, and each diplomatic mission in Vientiane was invited
by the Lao government to send one person on the flight. After
everyone else in the American Legation had declined, the invitation came down to me. I also declined, a fortunate decision
because the plane smashed into the side of a mountain, killing
all twenty-six on board.[5]

One year later, however, I defied the odds and accepted an
invitation for the inaugural Air Laos flight from Vientiane to Bangkok, a significant step for Laos in asserting its independence
from France. It was a special flight aboard a four-engine Boeing
307 Stratoliner that Air Laos must have bought at a bargain-
basement price. We boarded, strapped ourselves in, with real
seats and seat belts, but then the pilot announced that we had
a flat tire—the only time I have ever seen a flat tire on an air-
plane—and we all had to disembark. With the flat finally fixed,
we eventually took off on a flight that was uneventful, except
when one engine quit. All the Lao passengers laughed and thought
it was very funny, but I, the only non-Lao on board, did not think
it was so funny. I drowned my fears in good French champagne,
which was free and flowed freely during the flight. But as we
winged our way over the lush Thai countryside, whenever a bottle was emptied, the steward would open a side door in midair
and throw the bottle out. Bombs away!

Vientiane was a tropical post where we sweated eleven
months of the year but froze on the twelfth. For most of the
year, the weather in Laos made Washington's August weather
seem temperate by comparison, but we had a one-month cold
season in January, during which we froze because we were not
equipped with proper clothing or blankets. I recall driving my
Vespa motor scooter to work in the morning with one hand
to steer, and the other hand in my pocket to keep it warm,
and then, when the steering hand was about to freeze, I shifted
hands. At night, like a homeless person, I slept under newspapers rather than blankets. Since Laos had no newspapers,
I used the Paris *International Herald Tribune*, which came by
mail. And when we had no electricity, I would read my "blan-
ket" with the aid of a flashlight until I dozed off. The real challenge, however, was to take a shower during that cold month.
We had no hot water, but I learned that if I had two or three

---

[5] *New York Times*, 6 December 1954.

gimlet cocktails before dinner, I could jump into a cold shower and wash enough of myself to prepare for dinner.[6]

Vientiane was a tough post, physically and psychologically. We all suffered from heat rash. More serious tropical diseases were rampant, and medical evacuations frequent. The nearest civilian medical care was in Saigon, hours away by plane. Some left on stretchers, and others in straitjackets.

Local medical care was for emergencies only. The only European-trained Lao doctor in the entire country was the Minister of Public Health, Information, and Propaganda, but he was a gynecologist by training, a very fashionable specialty when he had studied in France. However, a small French military hospital with a few French army doctors was available for emergencies. Once, I had the temerity to visit a French Army dentist. Before beginning his examination, he poured gasoline into a portable generator to power his electric drill, and without washing the gasoline from his hands, put them into my mouth. I had not tasted gasoline since my earlier years in Germany when I often had to use a rubber tube to siphon gasoline into my car tank.

In Laos, it was far more interesting, as well as comfortable, to travel in the provinces and live more or less like the Lao people, sleeping in the homes of Lao officials, and dining on a rice-noodle dish called *khao poon*, a highly seasoned soup made from whatever was available locally.[7] I also bathed, as they did, in a river in early evening, clad only in a traditional black-and-white checkered cotton sarong, the men in one group and the women in another. I made many such trips into the countryside, and I learned enough Lao so that I could talk with people in the villages I visited, and where at times I had some interesting encounters.

One trip through Savannakhet province illustrated the declining role of France in Southeast Asia and its replacement by the United States. I was driving my reliable Land Rover through the jungle on a "road" that was little more than two ruts on a path, when I came to a crossing where I encountered a French Army Jeep in which were seated a US Army officer, a French

---

[6] A gimlet, easy to acquire a taste for, is like a dry martini but made with gin, Rose's Lime Juice, and a slice of fresh lemon or lime.

[7] For khao poon, place lightly sauteed rice noodles in a bowl, add thinly sliced raw vegetables, and cover with a thick broth made from fish, ground pork, and coconut milk.

officer, and a French Army driver. I approached and after reading the American's name badge on his chest, I exclaimed, "George, what are you doing here?" And he answered, "Yale, what are you doing here?"

He was Major George Jacobson, whom I had known when he was Captain Jacobson, Military Government Officer at Dachau, Germany, in the same military government unit where I was Executive Officer. Jacobson at that time was based in Saigon with the US Military Assistance and Advisory Group (MAAG), which provided hardware and advice to the South Vietnam Army. Years later, he was associate director of field operations in Saigon for the Agency for International Development, assistant for field operations to the American ambassador, and in 1975 in charge of evacuation plans at the American Embassy Saigon. One of the last Americans to leave Saigon, Jacobson left on a helicopter from the roof of the embassy before dawn on 30 April 30 1975 as North Vietnam tanks were preparing to move into the city.

On another trip, I dined with the French military. The French had troops in Luang Prabang, only ninety miles from the North Vietnam border, and when the commanding officer, a *commandant* (major), heard that there was an American in town, he invited me to lunch with his staff. It was like a scene out of a movie on the French Foreign Legion. It being a very hot day, as usual in Laos, we dined *en plein air* (outdoors), seated at a large table under a tarp to shield us from the sun. The conversation was cordial until the French major, speaking of the position of France in the world, commented that France was "caught between Russian communism and the American machine."

On another trip, I visited SENO, the French military base near Savannakhet, to attend the graduation ceremony of a class of Lao officer candidates.[8] It was there that I met another Lao prince, Boun Oum of Champassak, patriarch of the ruling family of southern Laos, who was to play an important role in the future of his country.

After the new Lao lieutenants were given their officer insignia, there was a traditional French *coupe de champagne*, and I must have lingered too long over my second or third "cup" because by the time I realized that I had not arranged for a

---

[8] SENO was a French acronym for the four corners of the compass—*Sud, Est, Nord, and Ouest.*

ride back to Savannakhet, most of the VIP guests had already departed. What to do?

A Jeep rolled by, and I flagged it down. "*À Savannakhet?*" I asked. "*Oui monsieur,*" said the Lao driver, and I hopped in. But, as the driver explained, he had to make another stop for a passenger, who turned out to be Prince Boun Oum. The Prince, a well-built man with an air of authority, took over the wheel of the Jeep, but not before he had buckled a US army web belt with a Colt .45-caliber pistol around his ample girth, and off we went to Savannakhet in a cloud of dust.

In a few minutes we caught up with the convoy of cars carrying the other official guests who were being escorted by truckloads of armed Lao soldiers at the head and foot of their convoy. But rather than join the convoy and take advantage of its security, Boun Oum stepped on the gas, overtook the convoy, and soon left it far behind.

"*Très mauvais ici*" (very bad here), said the Prince. "*La route?*" (the road), I asked. "*Non,*" he replied, "*les Vietminh.*" That part of the country was under the control of the communist Pathet Lao forces, and I never learned why he had chosen to pass up the security of the convoy and barrel unescorted down a road infested with Communist guerrillas, but it told me something about his personality and behavior.

A few years later, Boun Oum would play a key role in a political-military conflict with two other Lao princes that would eventually determine the future of their country. Boun would support Lao General Phoumi Nosavan, a southerner and cousin of Thai strongman Sarit Thanarat, who favored a Western-oriented, anti-communist Laos. Prince Souvanna Phouma sought a neutral Laos, and would be supported by a Lao military faction headed by Kong Le, a captain who staged a coup d'etat in 1960. Souvanna's half brother, Prince Souphanouvong, would continue to be leader of the communist Pathet Lao who were supported by North Vietnam. If you are still with me, that typified the political and internecine rivalries of Laos.

The other prince I knew, Savang Vattana, who later succeeded his father as king, abdicated after the communist takeover of Laos in May 1975, the same year in which Saigon fell to the North Vietnamese, and Cambodia to the Khmer Rouge. The king, his queen, and his young son, the new crown prince, would die three years later in a "reeducation camp" of the Pathet Lao.

In November 1955, Ted Tanen left Laos and was replaced as Country Public Affairs Officer by Fitzhugh Green. An advertising executive from New York's Madison Avenue, Green had worked on the Citizens for Eisenhower campaign and had come into USIA as a political appointee. Green had one big advantage—he spoke excellent French—but his New York advertising experience was not helpful in Laos. One of his early proposals, from which I was able to dissuade him, was to distribute among the Laotians baseball caps inscribed with anti-Communist slogans. But Green was a good jogging companion, and we would often jog together along the banks of the Mekong River. Once, as we took a midday jog, we ran past the home of Captain Jean Deuve, the chief French adviser to the Lao Security Service. The startled Deuve stared at us as we jogged by, probably thinking, "Mad dogs and Americans go out in the midday sun."

Our public diplomacy effort in Laos was intended to build national consciousness in a new country, a process which later came to be called "nation building." Eventually, we had an information center in Vientiane and branch posts in three provincial centers, each staffed by an American, in Luang Prabang, Savannakhet, and Pakse. Our modest program was the start of a soon-to-be massive American effort to maintain the independence of a small country whose people had been under foreign rule for most of their recent history.

When I left Vientiane in June 1956, two years after my arrival, there were more than a hundred Americans at the post, and the number was rapidly rising, eventually to reach more than a thousand. An independent and sovereign Laos had been established, but through no fault of its own it became caught up in the politics and violence of the Vietnam War. Laos would be in a state of continuing conflict for the next twenty years, a pawn in the rivalry between the superpowers.

Today Laos is nominally under a communist regime, but the United States has an embassy in Vientiane, and relations are cordial. Vientiane has grown from a sleepy town of some 20,000 to more than 600,000, and the population of Laos is now estimated to be 6 million. But recent visitors report that the Lao people have not changed much. They are still kind and hospitable, especially to Americans. And it's still *boh pen nyang.*

Chapter 3

BACK TO THE BOOKS

My reward for having served two difficult and dangerous, as well as productive, years in Laos was USIA's Meritorious Service Award and the offer of two years of Chinese language and area studies, the first year at the Foreign Service Institute (FSI) in Washington, and the second at an FSI school on Taiwan. I accepted the award but turned down the Chinese study.

Chinese language study was tempting, but an assignment in China was not possible at the time, nor in the then foreseeable future. As a Chinese-language officer, I would have had to look forward to future postings in places where there were large numbers of overseas Chinese—Singapore, Kuala Lumpur, Bangkok, Djakarta, Taiwan—but little chance of setting foot on Mainland China, as it was then called.

So I told my USIA personnel officer that I was too old to study Chinese—I was thirty-three at the time—but asked if there was an opening for Russian study. USIA, he replied, did not need anyone for Russian but I could have my choice of Czech, Hungarian, or Polish. That was interesting, and I asked for time to think it over while I attended Harvard Summer School on some of the annual leave I had accumulated over my many years abroad. Boston was my hometown, and a little exposure to academia seemed attractive after nine straight years abroad.

At Harvard, I took two courses: one on European intellectual history with Hans Kohn, and the other on American diplomatic history with Ernest May. May was at the start of a brilliant career, and Kohn was nearing the end of his, but I learned a lot from both. And it was Kohn who helped me to decide which language to study.

When I explained to Kohn that I had to choose between Czech, Hungarian, and Polish, he immediately recommended Polish. As he explained, Poland was the largest and most important of the East European countries, and the most important to the Democratic Party because of the large number of Polish-Americans in cities that were Democratic strongholds. That logic appealed to me, and I next had to decide where to study. But first, I had to make a loan to a Rockefeller.

One day, at the end of a class that ended at noon, one of my classmates, a pretty young woman, told me that she had left her purse at home and asked to borrow a dollar for lunch. "Sure," I said, as I gave her a dollar, "but what's your name," I asked. "Rockefeller," she replied. She repaid the loan the next day but without interest, and nothing further developed.

Harvard was a logical choice for my study, but in an interview there I learned that I would have to spend two years in Cambridge for an MA degree. Columbia, my second choice, told me that I could earn a master's in one year if I wrote a thesis, so off I went to Morningside Heights in New York City.

At Columbia, I took history courses with Oscar Halecki, the renowned Polish historian; government courses on Eastern Europe with Paul Zinner; and Polish language with Ludwik Krzyżanowski.[1] My thesis was on "The Development of German Policy Toward Poland, 1918–1921," which I researched by reading every issue of the *Frankfurter Zeitung* in the Columbia Library during those three years. Halecki was not pleased by my using only German sources, but when I explained that my German was fluent whereas my Polish was not, he relented and I received my MA in History in 1957.

Halecki, dean of Polish historians in exile, had been an *Endek* in Poland, a member of the National Democratic Party, the conservative party that was the principal opponent of the Polish Socialist Party. From Halecki I heard a version of Polish history that was quite different from what was being taught at

---

[1] Ludwik Krzyżanowski enjoyed telling the story of how, when he became a US citizen, an immigration official suggested that he change his name to one that Americans would be able to pronounce. Ludwik indignantly informed the official that a Krzyżanowski had fought in the Union Army during the Civil War and had reached the rank of brigadier general.

Polish universities in those years, and when I arrived in Warsaw, I thought it best not to disclose that I had studied with him. But, to my surprise, many of the Polish historians I encountered in Poland told me that they too had studied with Halecki, but at Warsaw University in the 1930s.

My nine months in New York were very pleasant. I had a small studio apartment on West 108th Street, close by Columbia University between Riverside Drive and Broadway. The music and theater in New York were great, and at night, after an evening of study I could go down to the corner kiosk and buy an early edition of the next day's *New York Times*. It was a great way to get reoriented toward the United States after being abroad for so many years.

After New York, it was back to Washington where a new assignment awaited me, but not in Poland as I had expected.

Chapter 4

A Voice to Vietnam

With my Polish studies completed, an assignment to Warsaw seemed assured, but for that I had to wait another year. USIA at that time had four positions in our Warsaw Embassy, but they were all filled and the person I had expected to replace decided to extend for another year. So, as often happens in the Foreign Service, I had to be "parked" somewhere for a year. And that's how my experience in Laos got me a position at the Voice of America (VOA) as Director of its Vietnamese Service.

The VOA assignment was not as strange as it may seem. South Vietnam and Laos had both been part of French Indochina, and while they were ethnically and linguistically distinct, the politics had some similarities. Both were new nations whose independence was supported by the United States, and both were threatened by communist North Vietnam. The Vietnam War had not yet begun, but its beginnings were festering and would soon erupt.

VOA is the radio voice of the US government to foreign audiences, and in those years it followed closely the policy set forth by the State Department. Every morning, Monday through Friday, VOA language service directors attended a meeting where guidance on how to report and comment on the day's news was discussed. The debate over VOA's independence in reporting the news that was to erupt in future years had not yet surfaced, and we faithfully followed the line set by State.

My staff at VOA consisted of two Americans—a news editor and a secretary—and seven Vietnamese. We all sat together in one large room, and in that room I had a microcosm of the cleavages dividing Vietnam. Some of my Vietnamese staffers were from the north, others the south, and still others from central Vietnam. Among them were Buddhists and Catholics, and perhaps some animists too, and some were family related. However, working together we produced two 30-minute, Vietnamese-language broadcasts a day, seven days a week. The first part was a 15-minute newscast devoted to news of the world and the United States, with special emphasis on topics related to Southeast Asia. The remainder of the broadcast consisted of features, taped in advance, on cultural, economic, and political subjects that might interest our audience. What held it all together was a remarkable young Vietnamese woman, Le Thi Bai—diminutive, beautiful, intelligent, and charming—whose melodious voice was known throughout Vietnam.

My year at VOA was uneventful and without surprises. It delayed by one year my entry into East European and Soviet affairs, but it provided experience in foreign broadcasting that proved invaluable during my later assignments in Warsaw and Moscow. And it enabled me to practice Public Diplomacy by speaking directly to an audience of millions in South and North Vietnam.

The only unexpected, but blessed, event was my marriage to Pamela Cheatham, a newly commissioned Foreign Service Officer at the State Department. However, as a consequence of regulations in force at the time, she had to resign from the Foreign Service upon becoming Mrs. Richmond. It was the Foreign Service's loss but my gain, as Pamela, with her political savvy and facility in learning languages, was to play an important and supportive role in my future assignments. And so, in June 1958 we winged our way to Warsaw for a three-year honeymoon at government expense.

Before departing for Warsaw, I wrote to the embassy asking if they could find work for my wife who, I pointed out, was a former Foreign Service Officer with good political sense and a facility for languages—in six months she would be speaking fluent Polish. Sometime after my arrival in Warsaw I found my letter in the embassy files. Someone had written on it, "Let her teach school."[1] It was again the embassy's loss but our gain, because we produced two children in Warsaw.

---

[1] That State Department policy on women Foreign Service Officers was not changed until 1972, when women who had been forced to resign were invited to rejoin the Foreign Service.

Chapter 5

POLAND—RUSSIA'S WINDOW
ON THE WEST

Poland has often been described as Russia's "Window on the West." That's because Poles, although a Slavic people, have been Roman Catholic since the tenth century, and culturally a part of Western Europe. Whether as an independent state or under Russian rule, whatever came to Poland from the West eventually found its way into Russia. That was true under Russian tsars in the nineteenth century, and under Soviet commissars in the twentieth.

Poland was also a very special country. As the Polish-Lithuanian Commonwealth in the Middle Ages it had been the largest country in Europe, holding sway over a vast domain extending from the Baltic to the Black Sea, and from present-day Germany almost to Smolensk in Russia.

In 1241 Poland saved much of Europe by absorbing the shock of a Mongol-Tatar invasion that threatened to overrun the entire continent. In 1683 Polish arms broke the Turkish siege of Vienna and halted the advance of the Ottoman Empire into Europe. In 1812 Poles formed the vanguard of Napoleon's march to Moscow, and protected the rear on his retreat. In the nineteenth century they fought for freedom in Belgium, Spain, the Balkans, and Italy; and in 1848 they fought with Hungarians for their independence. In World War I a Polish army fought with the Allies on the Western Front and suffered enormous casualties. And in World War II Polish armies fought in the Middle East, Russia, Africa, and Western Europe. Poles flew with the RAF in the Battle of Britain where one Polish squadron had the highest number of "kills" of any RAF squadron, shooting down nine German planes for every plane it lost. Poles landed in Normandy with the Allies and stormed Monte Cassino in Italy. And in Warsaw in 1944 the underground Polish Home Army held out for sixty-three days in an uprising against the Germans in which, before surrendering to superior forces, some 20,000 Polish fighters and several hundred thousand civilians were killed.

Poland has also had a special relationship with the United States. The first Poles came to the New World in 1608 as artisans with Captain John Smith at Virginia's Jamestown Colony. Tadeusz Kosciuszko, a professional military officer, served in the Continental Army in 1776 and was instrumental in its victories at Saratoga and West Point. Casimir Pulaski, a career cavalry officer, saved Washington's army at the Battle of Brandywine, and gave his life, at age thirty-one, leading a cavalry charge at Savannah; today, he is known as the father of the American cavalry. Poles also fought in the American Civil War, mostly with the Union Army.

During the Cold War, Poland had a communist government, was allied with the Soviet Union, and was a member of the Warsaw Pact. Its people, however, were anti-Russian and pro-American. As Poles like to tell it, Poland was like a radish—red on the outside, and white on the inside. When Eisenhower was elected US president in 1952, many Poles believed that the former general would liberate them from Soviet domination.

When Poland was partitioned in the late eighteenth century between Russia, Prussia, and Austria, Russia acquired by far the largest part, and with it some of Poland's western culture. But with the partitions, Poland was erased from the map of Europe for 123 years and ceased to exist as a sovereign state. The Russians, however, acquired control over a people who were difficult to rule and would be a source of future dissension, and at times rebellion, for both tsars and commissars.

When, in 1918, the three occupying empires all collapsed at the same time—Germany and Austria to defeat in World War I, and Russia to revolution—Poland reemerged as a sovereign state and enjoyed twenty-one years of independence until 1939. World War II brought a return to foreign rule, first by Nazi Germany, and then by communist Russia. By 1947, a Stalinist regime had been installed, and Poland was once more under Russian rule.

That ended in October 1956 when Poland had a change of government that replaced its Stalinist regime with one of national communism. The new Polish government, although still communist, ended the forced collectivization of agriculture, ceased overt harassment of the Catholic Church, restored academic freedom, and sought improved relations with the West. Poland remained within the Soviet Bloc, but its people enjoyed more internal freedom than any other member of the Warsaw Pact and it reestablished its historic cultural contacts with the West.[1] And that is how I came to practice Public Diplomacy in a communist country.

Warsaw, where I served as Cultural Officer from 1958 to 1961, was a very pleasant post. The cultural scene was rich and innovative, especially in music, theater, and literature. Moreover, I could talk with Poles, and I did not feel that I was working in a hostile environment.[2] Americans who served in Poland have liked the country and its people—their warmth and friendliness, regard for foreigners as guests of their country, and continuation of old customs such as kissing the hands of women. Some ten million Americans trace their origins to Poland, and a Pole you meet in Warsaw is likely to have a cousin in Chicago.

Poland, moreover, is the only country I have ever visited where the United States could do no wrong (although that certainty has been severely tested by the US war in Iraq). Former Polish ambassador to Washington Romuald Spasowski used to refer to State Department personnel who had served in Warsaw as "my Polish mafia."[3] I must have been considered a part of that mafia, because Warsaw was the best post in my thirty-year Foreign Service career.

Helping to make Warsaw pleasant were Ambassador Jacob D. "Jake" Beam and his wife, Margaret G. "Peggy." Beam, with prior service in Geneva, Berlin, London, Washington, Djakarta, Belgrade, and Moscow, brought to Warsaw a wide range of

---

[1] When Cardinal Stefan Wyszyński, the Polish Catholic Primate, was released from prison, he was personally escorted back to Warsaw by Zenon Klishko, the second ranking man in the new Polish Politburo.

[2] The only appointment I was ever refused was with Zenon Kliszko, the chief ideologist of the Politburo and close associate of party leader Gomułka.

[3] Spasowski served as a deputy foreign minister and was twice ambassador to Washington, but in December 1981, in protest against the imposition of martial law in Poland and the forcible dissolution of Solidarity, the free trade union, he resigned and was given refuge in the United States.

experience. Peggy had been a USIS Information Officer in Belgrade, where they met, and was familiar with what culture and information could do for US interests. Both of them were very supportive of our work.

Edward A. "Ed" Symans was chief of the embassy's Press and Cultural Section when I arrived in summer 1958. Symans, a Polish-American from Grand Rapids, Michigan, had been a student at Warsaw University in the 1930s, and was working as a clerk at our Warsaw Embassy when the Germans invaded in 1939. He next served with the State Department in Berlin, Moscow, Vladivostok, and Istanbul, and after the war ended, he had three assignments in Poland. Ed was fluent in Polish, and seemed to know everyone who was anybody in Poland where he served as our walking internet. You could walk into his office and ask what he knew about some Pole you had just met, and Ed, off the top of his head, would give you a complete rundown of the man's history and politics. When Symans left in 1959 we wondered how we could get along without him— but we did, which reminds me of an old saying: "If one man is indispensable in an organization, fire him."

The Polish language was at first a challenge but I soon learned that most of the Poles I dealt with also spoke French, German, or English, and we therefore had at least one western language in common. Moreover, when speaking Polish, I found that if I did not know a Polish word, I could take the French equivalent, add a Polish ending, and it would be understood and was often the very word I was looking for. And we ate well in Poland. With the end of collectivization and the return of private agriculture, almost everything essential was available in the public markets or private stores.

Cultural officers who served in Poland in those years had the novel experience of establishing a big cultural program in a communist country from the ground up. But in those years, USIA was a four-letter word in the Communist Bloc, and before winging my way to Warsaw I had to formally resign from the US Information Agency and be hired by State. That did not fool the Polish government, but they could honestly tell the Soviets that they were not allowing a USIA post to open in Warsaw.

Shortly after my arrival I called on the embassy political officer, Richard G. Johnson, and asked his advice on what was possible in Poland. "If you can show the Polish officials you work with," he replied, "that you really like Poland, you can do almost everything you want here." I followed that advice for the next three years, and success came easily.

Within a few years, many of the cultural activities considered normal in most countries had been established. The Ford and Rockefeller Foundations had led the way in 1957 by awarding fellowships to enable prominent Polish scholars, scientists, and cultural figures to study in the United States and Western Europe. The State Department and USIA followed with exchanges of graduate students, university lecturers, and performing artists; reopening an American library in Warsaw; providing assistance to English teaching programs; distributing US documentary films; and initiating direct exchanges between Polish and American universities. Other public diplomacy activities included publishing an illustrated monthly Polish-language magazine *Ameryka,* and establishing an International Visitor Program that brought Polish leaders to the United States, and a similar program for Americans to Poland.

In many of those activities, the American Embassy had the advantage of being able to use Polish *zlotys* accruing to the US government from the sale of surplus agricultural commodities to Poland under Public Law 480 ("Food for Peace").[4] That legislation provided long-term credit arrangements that enabled developing countries to purchase surplus US agricultural commodities at favorable terms. The Poles got the agricultural commodities they needed—wheat, feed grains, vegetable oils—and paid in zlotys that the American embassy used to cover its costs in Poland, including its cultural and information programs.

Another US law enabled agencies of the Polish government to purchase American books, periodicals, authors-rights, and commercial motion pictures under the Information Media Guaranty program, commonly known as IMG.[5] The Poles imported the media products, paid for them in zlotys, and the American exporter was paid in US dollars converted at a favorable rate by the US government. That enabled the Polish public to purchase American books in English, read bestsellers translated into Polish, and see recent Hollywood films in their local theaters and American plays performed in Polish on Polish stages. The IMG program in Poland ran through 1967 but

---

[4] TIAS 3999, exchange of notes, Warsaw, 12 February 1958.

[5] Title 1, P.L. 472, 80th Congress.

by the mid-1960s it had facilitated Polish purchases of nearly $7 million worth of US books, authors-rights, newspapers, periodicals, and films.[6]

Another advantage we had in working with Poles was their flexibility and tendency to seek accommodation rather than confrontation. Unlike a Russian *nyet,* which was usually firm and irrevocable, a Polish *nie* often led to a "maybe" if you talked a little longer at the negotiating table. And Poles seem to have difficulties in keeping secrets, so it was often easy to learn what would happen next.

We were once tipped off by a Pole that a demonstration against the Vietnam War was to take place in front of the American Embassy, but we were not given the exact time. When a crew from Polish Television pulled up and parked directly across from the embassy, I ventured forth and asked them what time the "spontaneous demonstration" would start. They laughed and gave me the exact time.

In such a hospitable atmosphere, Warsaw after 1956 was visited by many prominent Americans and artistic ensembles. Among those I had the pleasure of meeting were Senators Hubert H. Humphrey and Jacob Javits, Rep. Clement Zablocki, writers Saul Bellow and Mary McCarthy, presidential adviser Arthur M. Schlesinger Jr., pianist Artur Rubinstein, maestro Leopold Stokowski, MIT polymath Roman Jakobson, Yale history professor George Vernadsky, the sisters of John F. Kennedy, *New York Times* journalists James "Scotty" Reston and A.M."Abe" Rosenthal, the Ford Foundation's Shepard Stone, Leonard Bernstein and the New York Philharmonic, and the Juilliard String Quartet. Our most important visitor, however, was Vice President Richard Nixon in August 1959.

When Nixon stopped in Warsaw after his visit to Moscow, he was greeted by an effusive welcome from the Poles, much to the annoyance of the Polish government. Nixon's plane had landed at a military airport outside Warsaw where security was tight and crowds were prevented from gathering. But his route into the city had been broadcast by Radio Free Europe, and as his cavalcade approached the center of Warsaw the crowds grew thicker and more demonstrative. I was driving my Ford sedan a few cars behind Nixon's car, and in downtown Warsaw

---

[6] Wilson P. Dizard, Jr., *Inventing Public Diplomacy: The Story of the US Information Agency* (Boulder CO and London: Lynne Rienner Publishers, 2004), 164.

I had to stop to clear away bunches of flowers from the hood of my car so I could see where I was going.[7] In such a favorable environment, many things were possible in Public Diplomacy. Some of them will be described here.

In those years, we had little or no guidance from Washington on what to do in Poland, and didn't need any. Opportunities for Public Diplomacy were everywhere, funding was available, and all we had to do was establish the priorities.

Those were heady days, and Americans who served in Poland in those years can look back with satisfaction on a mission well accomplished. Moreover, although we did not know it at the time, much of our Public Diplomacy in Poland also found resonance in Russia, as Poland once more served as Russia's window on the west.

Margaret Schlauch and Academic Exchanges

Although USIA had four Americans in Warsaw when I arrived as Cultural Officer in July 1958, our cultural and information activities in Poland were still rather limited. USIA's "Wireless File," a daily electronic transmission of news and full texts of policy statements from Washington, was being distributed to the Polish media. An embassy film library had been opened, and USIA documentary films were being mailed on loan to viewers all over Poland. And an agreement would soon be signed to sell 30,000 copies of the illustrated monthly Polish-language magazine, *Ameryka,* produced by USIA in Washington. However, there were as yet no academic exchanges, mainly because none of the Warsaw Embassy staff had such experience in previous postings. Initiating an exchange of graduate students and university lecturers was therefore my first priority.

When I first proposed academic exchanges to Deputy Chief of Mission Frank G. Siscoe shortly after my arrival, he asked who would pay for the exchanges, and he seemed surprised when I replied that the State Department was prepared to do exactly that. That was rather typical of senior Foreign Service Officers at the time who had little knowledge and appreciation of the Fulbright program and other exchange activities of the

---

[7] The enthusiasm of the Polish people was not for Nixon personally but for the United States that he represented.

US Government, which later came to be known as a key component of Public Diplomacy.[8]

To Margaret Schlauch, an expatriate American who was head of the English Department at Warsaw University, goes much of the credit for resuming US academic exchanges with Poland. The Philadelphia-born, New York intellectual of German-Irish descent was a graduate of Barnard College, '18; Phi Beta Kappa member; Columbia University, MA, '19 and PhD, '27; New York University Professor of English, 1924 to 1950; world-renowned authority on Middle English, Chaucer, and Nordic literature; and member of many learned societies. Nine of her books are still in print. So how, one might ask, did Schlauch become a full professor at Warsaw University?[9]

Schlauch was the sister-in-law of Leopold Infeld, a Polish-born nuclear physicist who had worked with Albert Einstein at Princeton. Infeld, a naturalized Canadian citizen who had been teaching at the University of Toronto, left Canada with his wife in summer 1949 to visit Poland at the invitation of the Polish government. A few months later, the Infelds decided to remain permanently in Poland where he had been offered a position as Poland's top nuclear physicist. Schlauch's decision to leave New York for Warsaw was influenced, to some extent, by her desire to join her sister and brother-in-law, her only immediate family members, but politics and ideology also played a part.

In her letter of resignation to New York University, Schlauch wrote that her economic and political future in the US was "not auspicious, not even for a Chaucer specialist, if such a person has been and still is a Marxist (no matter how undogmatic) and doesn't intend to deny it."[10] In her letter, she also condemned US foreign policy and said she felt obliged to actively oppose it.

Prior to my arrival in Warsaw, Schlauch had no contact with the American Embassy, where she was regarded as a renegade. But after receiving the concurrence of Ambassador Beam, I called on her in autumn 1958 and asked what we together could do for American studies in Poland. Schlauch welcomed

---

[8] I later worked for Siscoe at the State Department where, as Director of the Soviet and East European Exchanges Staff, he was a strong supporter of exchanges.

[9] For a more complete account of Margaret Schlauch, see Yale Richmond, "Margaret Schlauch and American Studies in Poland During the Cold War," *The Polish Review* xliv (1999, no. 1), 53–57.

[10] *New York Times,* 6 February 1951.

my initiative—indeed she thought it was long overdue—and responded with two proposals. First, to establish an annual exchange of Polish and American graduate students, with at least one scholarship reserved each year for a Polish student of American literature or linguistics. Her second proposal was to exchange university lecturers—an American to teach literature in her department at Warsaw University, and a Pole to teach at an American university in a field designated by the two governments. I readily agreed to both proposals, and we set about to get the agreement of our governments. Approval was given quickly by Washington and Warsaw.

One year later we had an American lecturer, not in Warsaw as originally planned, but at Cracow's venerable Jagiellonian University where, as the Poles diplomatically explained to me, he would be less visible to the Soviet Embassy in Warsaw.[11] The following year, however, we were able to place a lecturer at Warsaw University: Hugh Gloster, by chance a former graduate student of Schlauch at New York University.[12]

In the following years more Fulbright lecturers in American studies were added at other Polish universities until there were as many as seventeen in various disciplines. And in 1971, Warsaw University's Institute of History hosted a Fulbright lecturer in American History, Wallace Farnham, the first postwar US lecturer in American history at a Polish university.

American studies continued to develop at Warsaw University where an American Studies Center was established in 1976 under a reciprocal arrangement with Indiana University which opened a Polish Studies Center in Bloomington the following year.[13] Leonard Baldyga and Robert Gosende of the American Embassy handled the negotiations with Warsaw, and I in Washington with Indiana.

In exchange for the American lecturers, the Polish government chose to send to the United States not lecturers but young Polish scholars to conduct research, half of them in sci-

---

[11] It was not until thirteen years later, in 1973, that Moscow would agree to a similar exchange of university lecturers with the United States.

[12] Gloster later was President of Morehouse College in Atlanta, Georgia.

[13] For an account of the founding of the Warsaw and Indiana centers, see Leonard J. Baldyga, "The 20th Anniversary of the American Studies Center at the University of Warsaw: An Historic Overview," in *Pochwala Historii Powszechnej* (Warsaw: Center for American Studies, 1996), 569–74.

ence and technology, and half in the humanities and social sciences.[14] Many of those Polish scholars went on to become professors in Polish universities.

The student exchange began in 1959 with four American and four Polish graduate students. One of the Polish students in that first year, Franciszek Lyra, was a student of Schlauch at Warsaw who three years later received a doctorate in American literature from Indiana University and became a lecturer in American Literature and English at Poland's Marie Curie-Skłodowska University in Lublin.[15] From 1992 to 2004, he was a professor at Warsaw University's Center for American Studies.

Margaret Schlauch, although an expatriate, was as American as apple pie. She had learned to speak Polish and was active in Warsaw's cultural and intellectual life, but she clearly missed New York and was homesick for America. She also had a weakness for martini cocktails, and each Christmas I would send her a package labeled "Do-It-Yourself Kit," containing gin, dry vermouth, and olives, all impossible to obtain in Warsaw at the time. And when the University of Michigan Symphonic Band came to Warsaw in 1961 and closed its concert with a rousing Sousa march and a medley of Michigan college songs, Schlauch joined other admirers from the audience, standing before the stage applauding wildly.

Schlauch was not politically active in Poland, and politics did not intrude in her classroom. Although she was a Marxist and differed with US foreign policy, in Polish academic circles she was a voice for liberalism and humanism. And like most intellectuals in Poland, she was disheartened when the hardliners among the Polish communists began to reassert their authority over Polish academic and cultural life.

In later years, her brother-in-law Leopold Infeld, to whom she was close, was one of thirty-four Polish professors and writers who signed a letter to the Polish prime minister protesting state censorship and calling for more cultural freedom. The letter was an attempt to halt the erosion of freedoms won in 1956, and to curtail the growing strength of the Communist

---

[14] That fifty-fifty is a distribution the Soviet Union would never agree to in its exchanges with the United States.

[15] Here, I am indebted to Franciszek Lyra's "American Studies in Poland," *American Studies International* (Spring 1978), 28–35.

Party's hardliners. That effort by Warsaw's intellectuals failed, but it was a preview of the epic struggle years later when the Solidarity movement emerged and triumphed.

After retiring in the late 1960s, Schlauch withdrew from public life. She visited the United States several times to lecture at the invitation of Americans who had been Fulbrighters in Warsaw. People who knew her in those years believe that she became progressively disillusioned by political events in Poland. Although not Jewish herself, she was shocked by the anti-Semitic purge of 1968 when most of Poland's few remaining Jews, many of them close friends of hers, were forced to emigrate. And in a curious turn of events, several of her former Warsaw students who left Poland in the 1968 exodus are now teaching at universities in the West.

In the last months of her life she was very ill, and it is not known whether she knew of the arrest for political reasons, only a few weeks before her death, of one of her successors as head of Warsaw University's English Department. That would have been her final disappointment with "People's Poland."

Schlauch died an American expatriate in Poland, but she bequeathed to her adopted country a rich legacy of American culture and scholarship. Thanks largely to her help, American studies were reestablished in communist Poland, an achievement that, in its place and time, took some courage. And far more than I had ever hoped, she helped to restore Poland's cultural and academic contacts with the United States.

Today, the Polish Fulbright Program is conducted by a binational commission funded by the two governments and established pursuant to an intergovernmental agreement signed in 1990. In the 2002–2003 academic year, it awarded some 125 grants to Polish and American students, researchers, university lecturers, and teachers. Warsaw's American Studies Center, which now has some 400 students, offers a master's degree and has exchange arrangements with several American universities in addition to Indiana. Lublin has a five-year program in American literature leading to the *habilitacja* (habilitation), Poland's highest academic degree and the prerequisite for becoming a university professor in Poland. There are also programs in American studies at universities in Gdańsk, Cracow, Łódź, Opole, Poznań, Sosnowiec, Toruń, and Wrocław.

In a celebration of the fortieth anniversary of the Fulbright program in Poland, Polish President Aleksander Kwaśniewski spoke of the role of the program in ending communism and preparing leaders in government, business, law, journalism, and other professions for the period of transformation to democracy and a market economy.[16] And as Franciszek Lyra, the first Polish Fulbrighter, put it, "We go to America to become better Europeans and better Poles. This notion evolved to turn into the core of the Fulbright Program."[17]

The American Library

Reopening an American library was the next task. There had been an American library in Warsaw after World War II, but it had been closed by the communist government in 1950. Ten years later, without fanfare, I opened a small library in the embassy for use by the Polish public. Emphasizing American studies and reference material, it was, at the time, the only library of its kind in Poland and was used mostly by university students and others interested in the United States. The library also received visitors and telephone calls from all over Poland seeking information on the United States, most often requests for names and addresses of US institutions with which some Pole wanted to make contact. Poles had no fears about visiting the American Embassy, and the Polish government made no efforts to inhibit such visits. To ensure the library's success, I hired as librarian the daughter of the Indian ambassador to Poland, a recent graduate of Cornell University, whose beauty and sari dresses attracted many visitors.

In 1992, the library was moved from the embassy to a former palace near Warsaw's Old Town. There it functioned as a library and cultural center until 1996 when declining USIA budgetary resources and high rent mandated its closing. However, its collection of more than 10,000 books was given to the American Studies Center at Warsaw University. And more recently the American library itself has come full circle, beginning anew as it had begun in 1960. It has been replaced by a state-of-the-art Information Resource Center (IRC) in the American Embassy—one of more than 100 such centers around the world, where a small staff of reference specialists, using computers

---

16 See http://www.fulbright.edu.pl/40-th.html

17 *The Warsaw Voice,* 31 October 1999.

and digital video equipment, responds to inquiries about the United States from the Polish government, academia, and the media. All that's missing is the books.

Book presentations were another aspect of my work as cultural officer, and they were a bibliophile's dream. Each week I received, via the diplomatic pouch, a copy of the Sunday *New York Times Book Review* for which I had carte blanche to order from USIA whatever I wanted, and with no limit on the number of books. My first priority was books for the embassy library—reference works and books on American literature and history. My second priority was books for Polish university libraries, which had a great need for foreign books but very little foreign currency to purchase them. For university libraries I would order one, two, or three or more copies of books that I thought would be useful.

The books arrived a few weeks later, also via the diplomatic pouch, and once every month I would fill the trunk of my car with books and head for a university library. One can imagine the welcome I received.

My favorite recipient for books was Brother Romuald, a Benedictine monk who was librarian at the Catholic University of Lublin, a university that the communist authorities had never closed down. Romuald spoke no English but he recognized a good book when he saw one. And if there was a duplicate copy of anything on my shelves, he would spot it and ask if he could have it. It was hard to say no.

Mary McCarthy and Saul Bellow

Books lead to authors, and a number of them visited Poland in those years on State Department grants. Among the more prominent during my more than three years in Warsaw were Mary McCarthy and Saul Bellow, whom we were fortunate to have for several weeks and at the same time in December 1959. They came as "American Specialists," the term used for Americans sent abroad by State as representatives of American culture, politics, and public affairs.

Mary McCarthy was scheduled to arrive by air but when the Warsaw airport was fogged in, her plane landed in Wrocław, a city in southwest Poland, from where the passengers were bussed to Warsaw. And that's when the embassy received a telephone call from her shortly after she had checked into Warsaw's Grand Hotel, which was not so grand.

One of a cultural officer's duties is to welcome prominent visitors. And so my boss, James R. West, the embassy's Public Affairs Officer, issued his order of the day. "Go to the Grand Hotel," he said, "and welcome Mary McCarthy to Poland." It was not a difficult task, and in a few minutes I was in her rooms at the hotel where she had settled with her husband, Bowden Broadwater III, and son, Reuel Wilson.[18]

I extended the customary greetings of the embassy and talked with her about our plans for her stay in Poland. When I returned to the embassy, West anxiously asked, "How was she?" "Devastating," I replied, "one of the most fascinating women I have ever met." West was also fascinated by McCarthy, and she by him, and after a whirlwind romance of one year, the two divorced their spouses and were married.

McCarthy was also attracted to Poland. As a Public Diplomatist, she met with Polish writers and lectured to Margaret Schlauch's students and Warsaw's PEN Club. In small meetings and dinners she also met a wide range of Polish intellectuals. In an interview published in *Nowa Kultura,* Poland"s leading cultural weekly at the time, she said, "My short stay in your country has created in me a feeling of emotion. In talking with people I gained the impression that I am renewing a conversation interrupted long ago. I regret that I came here for such a short visit. I would like to return here."[19] In expressing such sentiments, McCarthy may have been thinking of her Polish Jewish grandmother, about whom she wrote in her *Memories of a Catholic Girlhood.*[20]

Saul Bellow's visit to Poland was no less a success, although he was going through a divorce at the time and was not in the best of spirits. The future Nobel Laureate in Literature (1976)

---

[18] Reuel Wilson, a son by Mary's first husband, Edmund Wilson, the noted writer and literary critic, later studied at Jagiellonian University, became a Slavicist, and is today a professor at the University of Western Ontario.

[19] Cecylia Wojewoda, "A Talk with Mary McCarthy," in *Nowa Kultura* (Warsaw), 31 January 1960 (translator unknown), Vassar College Special Collections, Mary McCarthy Papers, f. 133.3.

[20] Mary McCarthy, *Memories of a Catholic Girlhood* (New York: Harvest, Hbj, 1957).

was not published in the Soviet Union at the time, but he was well known in Poland where his books, thanks to the IMG program, were available in Polish-language editions. In Warsaw, Bellow met with writers at small gatherings, and delivered a lecture in English to a standing-room-only audience in Warsaw University's main auditorium where he was introduced by Margaret Schlauch. In Cracow, he gave a talk at the local Writers Union.

My trip with Bellow to Cracow provided a rare opportunity for an author-reader encounter. On the overnight sleeper, Bellow had the lower berth in our compartment, reading his favorite English poet, William Blake, and I had the upper, reading his newly published *Henderson the Rain King*. Whenever I had a question about Bellow's book, I would lean out over my berth and ask, "Saul, what did you mean by this?" All I got in response was a friendly, knowing smile.

We also visited the nearby former German concentration camp at Oświęcim (Auschwitz) where there were no smiles, and we were deeply moved by the tragic reminder of the Holocaust. For those who question the existence of the Holocaust, a visit is recommended.

From Wall Street to Warsaw Streets

Another example of what was possible in Poland in those years came with a visit by Warren Phillips, CEO of Dow Jones, Inc. and publisher of the *Wall Street Journal*. Ambassador Beam gave a lunch for Phillips, and after the ambassador had given him a briefing on Poland, our visitor surprised us by asking, "Mr. Ambassador, what can the *Wall Street Journal* do for you?"

Beam turned to me and asked, "Yale, what can the *Wall Street Journal* do for us?" Somehow, I came up with a novel idea in Public Diplomacy. Poland had eighteen higher schools of economics, I told Phillips, similar to US graduate schools of economics and business administration, and I asked if he could give each a six-month subscription to the *Journal*.

"No problem," said Phillips, "just send me the mailing addresses," which I promptly did. And a few weeks later, when I visited the libraries of several of those economic schools, copies of the *Wall Street Journal* were prominently displayed on library racks alongside the Soviet dailies *Pravda* and *Izvestia*.

International Press and Book Clubs

Many things in Poland were neither red nor white, but gray. One example was the International Press and Book Clubs, a chain of reading rooms open to the public and maintained by the communist government in eighteen of Poland's major cities. There, Poles could read foreign magazines and newspapers, carefully selected but especially strong on the publications of foreign communist parties. On the racks one could find France's *l' Humanité*, Italy's *l'Unità*, London's *Morning Star*, and New York's *Daily Worker* (later, *Daily World*), all of which were eyeopeners for Poles because they reported much more than Soviet newspapers. But as I discovered on several visits to the Warsaw reading room, conveniently located on the corner of Nowy Świat and Aleje Jerozolimskie, Warsaw's main downtown intersection, there were also copies of Western non-Communist newspapers, including the Paris *International Herald Tribune*.

That prompted my call on the director of the reading rooms, Helena Michnik, and her deputy, a Mr. Wasilewski.[21] Michnik, a historian, was a handsome woman who spoke excellent English and looked like someone's Jewish aunt from the old Bronx. After initial pleasantries, I was given a briefing on the work of the Press and Book Clubs, after which I asked if she would like to have eighteen free subscriptions to *Time* and *Newsweek* for display in her reading rooms. "Why, of course," replied Mme Michnik with a big smile, as Mr. Wasilewski looked on glumly. USIA in Washington promptly arranged for the subscriptions, and when I checked several of the reading rooms a few weeks later, *Time* and *Newsweek* were prominently displayed.

A Soviet Salute

It's not often that an American cultural attaché gets to visit a Soviet army camp, but I was probably the first, and the last, to do so.

It was an election day in Poland, and accompanied by my wife, I was part of an embassy effort to see how the Poles were

---

[21] The charming Mme Michnik was the mother of Adam Michnik who later became a prominent dissident and democrat, and is today chief editor of *Gazeta Wyborcza*, Poland's leading daily newspaper.

going to the polls. In western Poland, where I was assigned to observe the elections, the Russians had several military camps, one of which I stumbled upon as I drove down a rural road. As I approached the camp entrance, I noticed a Soviet soldier, in baggy pants, peaked cap, and a Kalashnikov slung over his shoulder, standing guard by the gate.

Shto délatb? (What to do?), as the Russians would say. To come to a screeching halt and turn around would certainly have attracted the guard's attention, and perhaps a few rounds from his Kalashnikov. So I continued my slow approach to the camp, and the guard, impressed by my big blue Ford sedan, snapped to attention with a "present arms" salute as we drove by and entered the camp.

To make a quick exit would have attracted more attention, so I drove around the camp and exited as I had entered—with the guard again giving me a snappy salute—and relieved that I had not created a diplomatic incident. In retrospect, however, I missed an opportunity to conduct some Public Diplomacy with the Russians.

Socializing with Poles

Was it possible for an American diplomat to socialize with Poles and have Polish friends during the late 1950s? Like much else about Eastern Europe, the answer is yes and no.

Our social life was very active. For Americans who spoke Polish, there was plenty to do in the evenings, and Americans, like other foreigners, were able to take advantage of traditional Polish hospitality. But making friends was more difficult.

It was possible to invite Poles to our homes for cocktails or dinner, and they always came. But anything beyond that, or continued contacts, would arouse the suspicion of the UB, the Office of Security (Polish secret police), and could cause problems for our Polish acquaintances. That was especially true during the latter months of my three-year tour of duty in Warsaw, when the hardliners in the Party began to reassert themselves.

Some Poles had no hesitation in cultivating acquaintances with Americans and seemed to seek invitations to social functions at the embassy or our homes, but one had to wonder whether they were doing so at the behest of the UB, or merely taking advantage of our ample supply of alcohol and cigarettes. But even those contacts were useful since, if they were seeking information, they were usually willing to give some in exchange. And we could practice our Public Diplomacy on them by explaining US policy positions.

Polish Jews and Jewish Poles

The history of Poland is also a history of the Jews who lived in Poland for more than a thousand years. Their numbers greatly increased in the thirteenth century when, as victims of the Crusades in Western Europe, Jews found sanctuary in Poland where they were invited by Polish kings to aid in economic development. A charter in 1264 promised them complete freedom and opportunities for economic livelihood.

Again, in the fourteenth century when Jews in Western Europe were blamed for the bubonic plague—the Black Death (1348 to 1351) that left twenty-five million dead—Jews were invited by Polish King Casimir the Great to help settle the vast and mostly empty lands, newly taken by Poland from Tatar rule. With protection under law, more than half of world Jewry eventually found a home in the Polish-Lithuanian Commonwealth, a land of many nations, and ethnic and religious groups. For centuries, tolerant Poland was the home of world Jewry and, with fewer restrictions than anywhere else in Europe, the Jewish community multiplied and Jewish culture flourished.[22]

But the Commonwealth, as noted above, was partitioned in the late eighteenth century by its imperial neighbors—Austria, Prussia, and Russia—and Jews fared differently in the three parts, better in Prussia and Austria where, in the nineteenth century, they were granted equal rights under the law, but much less so in autocratic Russia that used anti-Semitism as a state weapon. And it was in Russia that Jews were restricted to the Pale of Settlement, a broad band of territory extending from Lithuania to the Black Sea, where they lived in largely Jewish towns and acted as middlemen between the landowning aristocrats and gentry, and the peasantry.

After World War I, nationalism emerged in the new Polish state, as elsewhere in Central Europe, and Jews were often

---

[22] Nor were Jews in Poland required to live in ghettos.

seen as an alien element. For the first time, Poles were a majority in their own country, and to be Polish was to be Catholic. Nevertheless, in the interwar period ten percent of Poland's population were Jews, and in Warsaw that figure reached 30 percent. Moreover, their influence greatly exceeded their numbers. Jews were prominent in many of the professions—law, medicine, literature, and journalism—as well as business, and the arts and crafts. Cultural assimilation in the cities was high, and many of those Polish Jews became Jewish Poles. And in a strange turn of history it was mostly Jews who had assimilated, who spoke Polish fluently without an accent and could pass for Poles, who survived the Holocaust in Poland.

Most of the Polish Jews were gone in 1958 when I arrived in Poland, victims of Hitler's "Final Solution" in which some three million of them perished, along with three million Poles. So it was with some surprise that I learned that among the survivors, Jews were prominent in many of the fields that were a part of my Public Diplomacy work—journalism, academia, literature, music, film, theater, and diplomacy. Some had managed to flee Poland after the German onslaught in 1939; others had the good fortune to be abroad when the war began, and still others had emerged from hiding. Those who had sought refuge in the Soviet Union returned with the victorious Soviet army. Others had spent the war years in England or with the Polish army that fought with the Allies in the West with great distinction. Altogether, some 200,000 Polish Jews fought against Nazi Germany in the ranks of Polish armies on Polish soil and in exile, many of them, due to their education, as officers.[23]

Many of the Jews who had spent the war years in the Soviet Union returned as communists, while many of those who had been in the West returned as members of the Polish Socialist Party (PPS). When, under Soviet direction, the small Polish Communist Party merged with the left wing of the much larger Socialist Party in 1948, they formed the Polish United Workers Party (PZPR), so named because communism had never had a large following in Poland, and most Poles could not be expected to vote for any party called communist. The socialists, since they outnumbered the communists, thought that they

---

[23] Benjamin Meirtchak, *Jews—Officers and Enlisted Men in the Polish Army, Prisoners of War in German Captivity 1939–1945* (Tel Aviv: Association of Jewish War Veterans of Polish Armies in Israel, 5 vols., 2003).

would be predominant in the new party. But they were mistaken and disillusioned when Poland became another satellite of the Soviet Union, and communists held the reins of power in government, the military, and the secret police. In 1949, a Soviet general of Polish origin, Konstantin Rokossovsky, was installed as Minister of Defense, Deputy Prime Minister, Commander-in-chief of Polish military forces, and member of the Polish Politburo, and Soviet advisers were spread through the armed forces and security apparatus.

In October 1956, however, a nationalist faction within the PZPR succeeded in ousting the pro-Soviet cadres. The new leadership, headed by Władysław Gomułka, a Polish communist who had been imprisoned during the Stalinist years, promised a "Polish road to socialism," which was much milder and had broad public support. As noted above, a new politburo, purged of Soviet stooges, halted the forced collectivization of agriculture, ended overt harassment of the Catholic Church, restored academic freedom, and sought economic and cultural contacts with the West.

But in 1968, most of the prominent Jews of Poland, and many thousands of others, were forced to flee the country in yet another anti-Semitic purge, organized this time by the Polish communist authorities. The purge came as part of a campaign against Polish dissident intellectuals and students who had joined the protest movement sweeping across Western Europe in that year. But it also came a year after the 1967 Israeli victory in the Middle East Six-Day War. Poles of Jewish origin were accused of being pro-Israel, and thousands left, never to return. Thirty years later, they were invited back by Polish President Aleksander Kwaśniewski, who called the 1968 anti-Semitic campaign a shameful page in Polish history.

Chapter 6

VIENNESE VIGNETTES

After more than three years in Warsaw, I was assigned to Vienna, Austria, in November 1961, to head USIA's Special Projects Office (SPO), a misnomer if there ever was one. In Soviet parlance, anything with the word "special" implied something secret or with an intelligence connection. That was not true of the Special Projects Office, a unit of USIS Vienna, although there was one rather unusual aspect of its work that I did not learn of until I arrived there.

During the Cold War Vienna had a well deserved reputation as a city of espionage and intrigue. Both the Soviet and American embassies had large intelligence sections, for the Soviets the KGB and GRU (military intelligence), and for the Americans the CIA. Their doings were not usually so dramatic as portrayed in the film, *The Third Man,* but there was often something going on behind the scenes that was not made public.

SPO's principal purpose was to provide support for the Public Diplomacy work of our embassies in Eastern Europe and the Soviet Union. To do that, we had a large and highly skilled Austrian staff that could prepare small photo exhibits on American themes, or larger exhibits for countries like Poland where such exhibits were possible. SPO also had a first-rate printing plant that could produce pamphlets and other printed material on short notice for distribution by our embassies in the East. And it had the largest photo archive in Austria, with photos from Eastern and Western Europe, and the United States, which were made available gratis to the Austrian and foreign press to embellish their articles.

Another SPO product was a Monday to Friday daily bulletin of news and feature stories from the radio broadcasts and print media of the East European satellites, as they were then rightly called. Austrian employees of SPO, fluent in the languages of Eastern Europe, would monitor radio newscasts from Albania, Bulgaria, Czechoslovakia, Hungary, Poland, and Romania, in the office during the day and at home in the evening. They would also scan the print media of those countries, which could be purchased in Vienna, and translate into German items that would be of interest to the Austrian press and correspondents of the Western media stationed in Vienna but whose "beat" was Eastern Europe.[1] Many Western publications found it more convenient, as well as comfortable, to base their correspondents in neutral Austria rather than in communist Eastern Europe, where living and working conditions were difficult, travel was often restricted, and where they could not always report what they wished.[2] SPO also maintained an extensive unclassified archive on the East European countries that was used by Western correspondents and visiting scholars.

The unusual aspect of SPO was a task that was not written into my job description, nor was it to be found in any classified document. SPO regularly received copies of classified reports from our embassies in Eastern Europe—telegrams as well as dispatches that came via the diplomatic pouch—and it was my job to leak selected contents to Western correspondents in Vienna, after having duly "sanitized" them by deleting references to embassy sources and other information whose confidentiality had to be protected. At my discretion I could leak information that was newsworthy and reflected unfavorably on the East European regimes but had not been made public by the communist-controlled press.

When I was briefed on that aspect of the job, I asked if Washington would protect me if I made a mistake and leaked something that I should not have. "No," was the response, I was on my own, and would have to suffer the consequences of any errors I made.

---

[1] The SPO daily bulletin was similar to the bulletin produced by the Foreign Broadcast Information Service, but distributed to recipients on the day of publication.

[2] Many of the news stories filed by Western correspondents from Vienna in those years with the lead, "Travelers from . . . report that . . .," were based on reports from SPO.

Fortunately, during my two years in Vienna I made no errors, although I had a close call once. To M.S. "Mike" Handler, the veteran *New York Times* correspondent in Vienna, I had given excerpts, duly sanitized, from a dispatch of our Budapest Legation. Based on that dispatch, Handler filed a story that was published in the *Times*. But a few days later, Budapest informed me that something in the Handler story was in error. What to do?

I so informed Handler, and he came up with a ruse to protect himself and the *Times*, and enable him to maintain the confidence of his contacts in Hungary. At his suggestion, I made a visit to the *Times* office in Vienna and, in a room that Handler believed was bugged, I informed him that the information on which he had based his story was in error. That "confession" of mine got him and the *Times* off the hook and enabled him to maintain the confidence of his contacts in Hungary and continue his respected reporting.

Vienna in those years, as noted above, was home base for many Western correspondents whose beat was Eastern Europe. Among the more prominent, in addition to Handler, were Clyde Farnsworth (*New York Times*, who succeeded Handler), Nora Beloff (*London Observer*), Ernst Halperin (*Neue Zürcher Zeitung*), Dino Frescobaldi (*La Stampa*), Eric Bourne (*Christian Science Monitor*), and Paul Lendvai (Austrian newspapers).

Life in Vienna was *gemütlich,* but uneventful and less interesting than Warsaw. Poland was much larger than Austria, but in Warsaw it was possible to know many important people and to learn what was going on behind the scenes. In addition, the Poles were very innovative in the arts, and there was always something new to see. And in Poland, it was always interesting to follow the latest episode in the continuing standoff between the communist government and the Polish people.

Austria, by contrast, recalling its former imperial glory, appeared to be living in the past, and the city of Vienna seemed to be one big museum. Often, the news of the day was the latest round in the sparring between the two major parties, the conservative People's Party and the left-of-center Austrian Socialist Party, which together cohabited the government and divided the spoils.

What was missing in Vienna was the Jews who had provided much of the creativity in Vienna's prewar music, theater, arts, journalism, and literature. As my landlady, Frau Baronin von Wieser, once told me, "The Jews provided the spice that made Vienna so appetizing."

But Vienna, like Poland, also had history everywhere. I lived in Grinzing, a suburb on the edge of the city, amid the vineyards and *Weinstuben* (wine taverns) where the Viennese and their visitors spend evenings at a *Heurigen* (literally, this year's wine), sampling the local wines, dining on delicacies, and listening to the traditional music of Vienna played by local musicians. Just down the street from our apartment on Schreiberweg was Nußdorf, where Beethoven had lived. And not far from Grinzing was the *Türkenschanz* where the Turks had encamped during their siege of Vienna in 1683. From my kitchen window I could see the Kahlenberg, the hill on the edge of the city, and the famed Vienna Woods; and from my living room, on a clear day, I could see the snow-covered Alps.

More difficult to see was the Vienna Philharmonic. Season tickets were sold out far in advance, and were often handed down within families from generation to generation. During my two years in Vienna, I managed to attend only one Philharmonic concert, and that was when the good Frau Baronin let me and my wife use her season ticket for a Sunday morning concert.

The Vienna State Opera, another gem of the Viennese musical world, was easier to attend. When I arrived in Vienna, the American ambassador still held the royal box at the Opera, a relic of the early postwar years when the Opera was located in the American sector of a Vienna occupied by the victorious four powers. Embassy staffers could call the ambassador's secretary late in the afternoon and inquire if there were any seats that evening that were not being held for the ambassador's guests or official visitors from Washington. But H. Freeman Matthews, who was ambassador when I arrived, decided that, since Austria was no longer an occupied country, it was not appropriate for the Americans to have a hold on the royal box, and he gave it up. However, with those royal seats gone, it was still possible to purchase a *Stehplatz* (standing place) just prior to a performance, and see and hear an opera while standing in the rear of the theater until you spied an empty seat somewhere in the hall.

What made Vienna somewhat more interesting was the steady stream of prominent visitors, transiting to or from Eastern Europe and the Soviet Union, who stopped in Vienna to savor the music, charm, and ambiance of that lovely city on the Danube.

One prominent visitor in 1961 was Edward "Ted" Kennedy who, as a candidate for the US Senate, was on his way to Poland. The Kennedy family had long had a special relationship with Poland, due in part to the marriage of Jacqueline Kennedy's sister into the Polish Radziwiłł family. The Kennedy party was scheduled for a few hours layover at the Vienna airport to connect with a flight to Warsaw, and Ambassador Matthews, who had worked for Kennedy's father when the latter was ambassador in London, gave a lunch at the airport for the young Kennedy. I was seated next to Kennedy so I could brief him on Poland.

As I was explaining to Kennedy that the two most powerful men in Poland were Władysław Gomułka, head of the communist party, and Stefan Cardinal Wyszyński, primate of the Catholic Church, we received news that the flight to Warsaw had been cancelled due to bad weather over the Tatra Mountains. Kennedy, demonstrating his clan's boldness and disregard of danger, immediately instructed one of his aides to hire a private plane, and after lunch he winged his way to Warsaw despite the wicked weather.

A more entertaining visitor was Nicolas Slonimsky—musicologist, conductor, composer, Harvard professor, author, and bon vivant. The St. Petersburg-born Slonimsky had lectured for the State Department in the Soviet Union, Poland, and other East European countries, and was spending a few days in Vienna, resting and recuperating from his travels and travails. We invited him to dinner at our apartment, after which he entertained us by playing the Johann Strauss "Blue Danube Waltz," in his own arrangement for two hands and two feet, and on our landlady's beautiful Bösendorfer grand piano on which Brahms had played. At age sixty-eight, the still agile Slonimsky had no trouble raising his legs to pound his heels, along with his hands, on the keyboard. Fortunately, our landlady was not one of our guests that evening.

During my two years in Vienna I was able to visit all of our posts in the East that I had not yet seen. With an eye toward a possible future assignment, I found Prague beautiful but closed to US cultural and information activities. Budapest, likewise beautiful, was also closed, since Cardinal Mindszenty, the Catholic primate of Hungary, was still in residence at the

American Legation where he had been given refuge during the 1956 Hungarian Revolution. Bucharest was grim and likewise not yet ready for USIS activities. And Sofia, under Communist dictator Todor Zhivkov, was clearly the end of the line. Moscow, however, personifying power and intrigue, peaked my interest. Since 1958, the United States had a cultural agreement with the Soviet Union that permitted a wide range of cultural and informational activities. Clearly, Moscow was a future post for me, and I began to study Russian in Vienna with a private tutor.

A reminder of the proximity of the Soviet Union, and Vienna's exposed position, came in August 1968 with the Cuban Missile Crisis. World attention was focused on Cuba where the two superpowers were engaged in a standoff. But in Austria, American Embassy personnel were preparing to evacuate Vienna. We were instructed to tank up our private cars, prepare small travel bags for family members, and be ready to join a vehicle convoy headed for Italy via the Brenner Pass. It was a chilling reminder that the Cold War could easily turn into a hot war.

Toward the end of my tour in Vienna, I had a visit by Frank G. Siscoe, who had been deputy chief of mission in Warsaw when I was stationed there. Siscoe had been appointed Director of the Soviet and East European Exchanges Staff at the State Department, and he asked if I was interested in coming to work with him in Washington. I accepted, and thus began another episode in my Cold War odyssey.

Chapter 7

EAST EUROPEAN EXCHANGES

The Soviet and East European Exchanges Staff, where I worked at the Department of State 1963–1966, was the office responsible for the political and security aspects of US exchanges with the Soviet Union and the countries of Eastern Europe. It was an important element in our public diplomacy effort during the Cold War to end the Soviet Bloc's self-imposed isolation and engage it in cooperative activities. EUR/SES, as the office was known at State, had a staff of twelve, and was in the Bureau of European Affairs (EUR), the political bureau, rather than the Bureau of Educational and Cultural Affairs (CU). Its main task was monitoring US exchanges with the Soviet Union and Eastern Europe, including the screening of visa applications of citizens from those countries coming to the United States on exchanges.

After the death of Joseph Stalin in 1953, the Soviet Union began to show some interest in cultural and scientific exchanges with the West. At the Geneva Foreign Ministers Conference in October 1955, the United States, Britain, and France presented a seventeen-point proposal to remove obstacles to exchanges in culture, education, the information media, books and publications, science, sports, and tourism. Soviet Foreign Minister Vyacheslav Molotov rejected the initiative but indicated that the Soviet Union might be interested in concluding bilateral agreements on some of those activities. Further developments came in 1956 when Nikita Khrushchev, in his secret speech to the Twentieth Congress of the Communist Party of the Soviet Union, criticized Stalin and called for a new policy of "peaceful coexistence" and increased contacts with the West. Two years later, the United States and the Soviet Union signed the first in a series of intergovernmental agreements for exchanges in culture, education, science, technology, and other fields. Commonly called the Cultural Agreement, its watchwords were equality, reciprocity, and mutual benefit.[1] The East European countries eventually followed the Soviet leadership, some with and others without formal agreements with the United States. But as exchanges with the Soviet Bloc proliferated, the US government had to devise procedures for the arrival of large numbers of exchange visitors from those countries, and how to respond to the growing interest of US governmental and non-governmental agencies and private organizations desiring to participate in the exchanges.

A major problem was how to issue visas to Soviet and East European visitors who would otherwise be ineligible for admission to the United States under existing legislation. Another consideration was how to ensure that the exchanges, especially those in science and technology, would not be used by the Soviet Bloc countries to access information that might impinge on US national security. The exchanges had strong support from President Eisenhower, the US Congress, and the public at large, but only a few years had elapsed since the anti-communist McCarthy hearings, and measures had to be taken to ensure that the exchanges would not be misused by the Soviets.[2]

With the establishment of EUR/SES, a new category of visas for Soviet and East European exchange visitors was created, "Special Exchange," with the acronym SPLEX tagged to the visa of every exchange visitor from the Soviet Bloc. For each SPLEX visa applicant, the field of study and proposed itinerary in the United States were checked out by EUR/SES, in advance of visa issuance, with various components of the US intelligence community. A Committee on Exchanges (COMEX), representing the intelligence and technical security communities, as well as other government agencies concerned with exchanges, reviewed the subject of study or research and proposed itinerary in the

---

[1] For more on the Cultural Agreement, see Yale Richmond, *Cultural Exchange and the Cold War: Raising the Iron Curtain* (University Park, PA: Pennsylvania State University Press, 2003), 14–20.

[2] Eisenhower, in particular, was a strong supporter of people-to-people exchanges.

United States. COMEX rendered an advisory opinion to the State Department as to whether the proposed visit was in a field considered sensitive to US security interests, and whether the visit would result in a net intelligence loss or gain, i.e., would the visiting scientist learn more from us than we would learn from him?[3]

In cases where a visitor's research was in a field that might negatively impact US security, we could deny the visa. But since exchanges, in principle, were found to be in the US national interest, in most such cases the visitor's proposed US itinerary could be adjusted to ensure that there was no access to research funded by the Department of Defense. Moreover, the itineraries of Soviet exchange visitors within the United States were monitored, and any deviation from an approved itinerary required advance notification to EUR/SES.

All Soviet visa applicants traveling on official passports, which was almost always the practice, and declining to appear for an interview with a US consul, also the usual case, were routinely found ineligible for a visa under US immigration legislation in effect at the time.[4] However, a waiver of visa ineligibility could be issued by the Department of Justice if the Department of State, after considering the recommendation of COMEX, found the visit to be in the national interest. As it turned out in practice, few visitors were found ineligible, and in most of the questionable cases, it was possible to change the place of study or itinerary and find the visit to be in the national interest. Moreover, visits to production facilities were normally not permitted. And since pure science is universal and has no secrets, it was in production that the United States was usually ahead of the Soviet Union and where sensitive technology had to be protected from intruding Soviet eyes.

For East European exchange visitors, there were fewer strictures but they were similarly screened by the intelligence community since there was always the possibility that they could be acting for the Soviets. Poland, Hungary, and Czecho-

---

[3] Represented on COMEX, a subcommittee of the Technology Transfer Intelligence Committee (TTIC), were CIA, FBI, Defense Intelligence Agency (DIA); Air Force, Army, and Naval Intelligence; National Security Agency (NSA); and Departments of Commerce, Defense, Energy, Justice, State, and Treasury, and USIA. COMEX was chaired by the CIA until 1982, and by DIA until 1994 when it was disbanded.

[4] Immigration and Nationality Act of 1952 (McCarran-Walter), as amended.

slovakia had big scientific communities, and scientists and scholars from those countries were often sought by American universities and research institutions. From each of those three countries, at any one time, we might have several hundred exchange visitors in the United States. Romania, with which the United States by that time had an intergovernmental exchange agreement, was a special case, although the number of visitors from Romania was not large because the Romanian *Securitate* was very careful about whom they let out of the country. Bulgaria, the smallest of our five countries, had the smallest number of exchange visitors, although their caliber was uniformly high and they were usually experts in their fields.

My job title, in State Department jargon, was Supervisory Foreign Affairs Officer, which in practical terms meant that I had another Foreign Service Officer working under me, and together we covered Poland, Czechoslovakia, Hungary, Romania, and Bulgaria.[5]

One advantage of being in charge of East European exchanges was that I was on the list of invitees to functions at the East European embassies in Washington. It was a continuing round of *gulyas* with the Hungarians, *bigos* with the Poles, *knedlicky* with the Czechs, *mamaliga* with the Romanians, and *shopska salata* with the Bulgarians. And it was at a Romanian embassy lunch that I had my first encounter with Richard Perle, then a staffer at the Senate Foreign Relations Committee, who was later to achieve prominence as a defense hawk and critic of exchanges during the Reagan and George H.W. Bush administrations.

Guests were seated on two sides of a long table according to their protocol rank, and I, as the lowest-ranking US official, was seated at the end of the table. Seated opposite me was a short, rotund American whom I did not know. He asked what I did, and when I told him that I worked on East European exchanges at State, we got into a long and animated discussion, with my luncheon companion criticizing exchanges, and I defending them. After a while, when talk among others at the table had ceased and I realized that they were all listening to our conversation, I figured that my table partner must be

---

[5] Yugoslavia was not considered as within the Soviet Bloc, and its exchangees were not subject to SPLEX procedures. With the German Democratic Republic and Albania there were no exchanges with the United States in those years.

someone important, although Perle was only a Senate staffer in the 1960s.

More congenial acquaintances at the Romanian Embassy were its cultural attaché Ovidiu Popescu, an orthopedic surgeon by profession, and his wife, a dentist. I saw quite a bit of them, professionally because we had good relations with Romania, and Popescu often needed help in finding his way through the US government bureaucracy and private sector, and socially because they were both so charming. What Balkan intrigue, I wondered, had brought an orthopedic surgeon to Washington as cultural attaché, and when I asked him, Popescu explained it to me: The Romanian foreign minister had once been injured in a serious auto accident, and Popescu had helped him make a full recovery. When the minister, in gratitude, asked what he could do for him, Popescu replied that he would like to be cultural attaché in Washington. So much for Balkan intrigue.

Mine was a humdrum job but someone had to do it, and I was well qualified, having previously worked on exchanges in Poland. US policy encouraged exchanges with Eastern Europe, and I did my best to do that by offering encouragement and advice to various US government agencies and private organizations that wanted to invite an East European or Soviet to come and work or consult with them but did not know how to go about it. By providing such advice, we were promoting Public Diplomacy, not only with the exchange visitors, but also with their American hosts. And we were expanding the network of East Europeans who came, saw, and were conquered.

Wasserburg am Inn—Beers for Buergermeisters, 1950.

Hunting Wildschwein (wild boar) in Schweinfurt, 1950.

Schweinfurt, Left to Right—Oberbuergermeister Ignaz Schoen, Yale Richmond, US Land Commissioner for Bavaria George N. Shuster, Chief Judge C.F.W. Behl, 1950.

Georg Schaefer, head of KugelFischer, resides at "roof raising" of housing for workers built with Marshall Plan funds, Schweinfurt 1950.

Ambassador Charles W. Yost presents check for $2 million to Lao Prime Minister Katay Don Sasorith, Vientiane, 1955.

John Foster Dulles with Prince Souvanna Phouma, Vientiane, 1955.

John Foster Dulles practices Public Diplomacy, Vientiane, 1955.

Yale Richmond
as photographer,
Laos, 1956.

Air Laos flight, Economy Class, 1955.

Vice President Richard Nixon arrives in Warsaw, 1959.

Polish beauty reads Ameryka Magazine, Warsaw.

American Guide addresses audience in Russian at US National Exhibition, Moscow 1959.

Russians read Amerika Magazine, Moscow.

Amerika Magazine goes on sale, Moscow.

Russians sample free Pepsi Cola at the US National Exhibition Moscow 1959.

Russians and Kazakhs line up for entry to the USIA exhibition, "Graphic Arts-USA" in Alma Ata, Kazhakstan.

Chapter 8

MOSCOW AND MORE

Moscow was a most unusual Foreign Service post. An assignment there was good for your career, and you could learn a lot about Russia and the Soviet Union, but there was not much that an American diplomat could do there to sway the mighty Russian colossus. Contacts with Soviet officials were limited, and those we were able to see did not make policy. Also limited were contacts with the Russian public, and any Russians we were able to befriend ran the risk of harassment by the KGB. Moreover, my 1967–1969 tour of duty took place when Russia was ruled by a gerontocracy headed by Leonid Ilyich Brezhnev, who was not in good health. Those years, consequently, have come to be known by Russians as the "years of stagnation."

Despite the stagnation, a Moscow assignment provided an opportunity to see how the Soviet Union worked—or more often, did not work—to learn how things were done there, and how much of the old Russia still influenced what Soviet leaders thought and did. Like the old Russia, the Soviet Union had a highly centralized government, a powerful secret police, a pervasive ideology, a systemic censorship, an obsession with secrecy, a distrust of the West, and a tendency to use force to achieve its objectives.

Moscow was great preparation for future and more important assignments, and four of the officers I served with there eventually became ambassadors in other parts of the world. But perhaps the most important thing learned from a tour of duty there was that the Soviets were not ten feet tall. Soviet power was greatly overestimated by politicians and analysts working in Washington who had never served in Russia or even visited it. With some exceptions, such as nuclear weapons, the Soviet Union, like Tsarist Russia, was many years behind the West in its development. Soviet citizens were being exhorted by their leaders to overtake the West, and the United States in particular. That gave rise to a Soviet *anekdot* (as Russian jokes are called), that Russians should not overtake the United States because then Americans would see that Russian behinds are bare.

There were USIA cultural officers in Moscow—and that's no joke—and they were practicing Public Diplomacy. The Soviet Union regarded cultural relations and the broad range of exchanges and other activities they included as important elements in bilateral relations. And since reciprocity was an underlying requirement for the exchanges, it was therefore willing to permit the United States to conduct certain cultural activities in the Soviet Union in exchange for the right to do so in the United States. It was an eye for an eye, if not always a truth for a truth.

The objectives on both sides were not dissimilar. Each government wanted to tell its "story" to the people of the other country, promote its cultural achievements, and encourage the study of its language. And it was a two-way street because through cultural exchange we learned much about each other.

Politics also influenced cultural exchange. In the Soviet Bloc the dividing line between culture and politics was blurred, and the work of a cultural officer was often as much political as cultural. While the immediate objective may have been improved mutual understanding, the long-range objective was a more stable political relationship between the two countries.

For the United States, the political objective was to broaden communication in the hope of encouraging constructive change in the Soviet Union that would lead to more cooperation and less confrontation, and a relationship in which we would work together to resolve differences and avoid nuclear war. The latter objective was paramount, since each country had the capability to destroy the other, and the rest of the world as well.

An ambitious agenda? Yes, and one that offered no quick fixes or short-range solutions. It was a long-range agenda, in which cultural officers played a central, but not very visible, role that will be discussed in this chapter.

What did an American cultural officer do in a country that regarded the United States as an adversary, where practically all cultural and educational activities were controlled by a government committed to an ideological struggle with the United States, and where America was regarded with great suspicion, aggravated by envy? Moreover, during my years in Moscow an escalation of the Vietnam War, which Soviet propagandists never let us forget, presented another obstacle.

Much of our time was spent in carrying out the American side of the US-Soviet cultural agreement, and for that we needed, and received, little guidance from Washington. Scholarly exchanges were administered by the International Research and Exchanges Board (IREX), the non-governmental organization that represented the US academic community. IREX exchanges did not require much attention, except when an American student or scholar got into trouble and had to be recalled by IREX pronto for his own good, and before a minor infraction developed into a bone of contention between the two superpowers. But other exchanges under the agreement did require our attention—the big American exhibitions, visits by US performing artists, our monthly *Amerika* magazine, and the numerous delegations and individuals in various fields that came to meet with their Soviet counterparts. Some of those activities will be described in the following pages.

State control over information was pervasive, and what the Soviet public learned about the United States from the official media was limited by censorship, although the Russian people, in general, had a favorable attitude toward the United States despite decades of anti-American propaganda in their media. Soviet citizens knew that neither Russia nor the Soviet Union had ever had a war with the United States, and that we were allies against a common enemy, Germany, in two World Wars. Moreover, the Soviet people recalled the aid sent by the United States in the early 1920s to help them survive a famine, in the 1930s to assist in industrializing and in fulfilling their first Five Year Plan, and in the 1940s to help defeat Nazi Germany. US cultural programs in the Soviet Union built on that base of popular goodwill despite a government that was very cautious about contacts with the West.[1]

---

[1] The easiest way to get a sounding on the Russian "man on the street," I learned, was to stop my Plymouth station wagon in downtown Moscow, raise

Moscow, where I served as Counselor for Press and Culture, was considered a good assignment for USIA officers during the Cold War, but only a few made it. The staffs in Moscow and Leningrad (now St. Petersburg) were small, there were few positions for cultural officers to fill, and a working knowledge of the Russian language was required.

While there was not much that foreign diplomats in Moscow could do to sway the Soviet colossus, an assignment there provided a unique opportunity to learn much about Russia and Soviet communism—its weaknesses as well as its strengths—to separate fact from fiction about the West's main adversary, and to keep the US-Soviet relationship on an even keel when every issue in bilateral relations had the potential to escalate to a major confrontation between the two superpowers. When Llewellyn E. Thompson, on retiring at the end of his second tour as US ambassador to Moscow, was asked what his greatest accomplishment was, the veteran diplomat replied, "That I didn't make things any worse."[2]

Change, however, did come to Moscow, but very slowly in those years. Thompson often said that during his first tour in Moscow as ambassador (1957–1962), he was the only one in the embassy who had useful contacts with Russians, and his were at the top, with Nikita Khrushchev. By contrast, Thompson noted, during his second tour (1966–1968), the mid- and senior-level embassy officers had good Russian contacts, while he had none. That happened, in part, because in 1968 the Soviets decided that it would be useful for their Foreign Ministry officials working on China, Africa, Latin America, and other parts of the world to have contacts with foreign diplomats working on those same areas. Thus, the China specialist in the American Embassy found that Soviet officials working on China in the Ministry of Foreign Affairs were now willing to meet with him and exchange views.

Thompson's close contacts with Khrushchev have been documented by historian David Mayers:

> Their families enjoyed weekend retreats together at Khrushchev's dacha....These unprecedented occasions mixed business with

---

the hood, and start tinkering with the engine. I would soon be surrounded by a crowd of friendly Russians inquiring about the car, how much it cost, how fast it could go, and how many "horses" it had.

[2] In Thompson's final briefing for American correspondents in Moscow, a meeting the author attended.

pleasure. Hikes in the countryside, chirping children, boat out-
ings, and discussions of household matters competed with de-
bates over the merits of socialism versus capitalism or reviews of
matters of state.[3]

By contrast, adds Mayers of Thompson's second tour, "During his two-year assignment, he was mostly bored, was often
sick, and felt that he was wasting time.... In contrast to the
days of Khrushchev, he lacked entrée to the Kremlin...."[4]

For the ambassador and his staff, Moscow was indeed a
hardship post. Apartments and telephones were bugged, and
KGB harassment made working and living conditions difficult.
That became especially so in 1986, when all Russian employees of the American Embassy were withdrawn by the Soviet
government in retaliation for the US expulsion of Soviet personnel assigned to the United Nations in New York. All routine
housekeeping and administration at the Moscow embassy had
to be performed by the American staff, including such tasks as
shoveling snow, loading and unloading trucks, washing floors,
and cleaning toilets.

Housing in Moscow for Americans was adequate but far
less comfortable than in the United States. Food on the table
was limited to what could be purchased at local markets or
imported from Western Europe or Finland at increased cost.
There was an Anglo-American School, run jointly by the American and British Embassies, but it went only through grade 10,
and high school juniors and seniors had to attend school elsewhere, separated from their families. On the other hand, en-
rollment in Soviet schools was possible, and youngsters who
could cope with the rigid and regimented system of education
could acquire near fluency in Russian. It was possible to enroll
my ten-year-old daughter at Moscow's prestigious Gnessin Institute of Music where she received an excellent music education, studied flute part time, and received a prized *pyatyorka*
(five), the highest grade. And for her music studies at home,
we were able to rent an upright piano from the UPDK (Main
Administration for Service to the Diplomatic Corps) of the
Ministry of Foreign Affairs. No ordinary piano, it was an East
German Bluethner in excellent condition, and it came at the

---

[3] David Mayers, *The Ambassadors and America's Soviet Policy* (New York and
Oxford: Oxford University Press, 1995), 202.

[4] Ibid., 220.

bargain basement price of fifteen rubles ($21.40 at the official rate) a quarter, with no charge for delivery.[5] Whether it was bugged, we never learned.

Weather in Moscow was worrisome. Summers could be very hot, and activity slowed in August when many Russians took their vacations at the family dacha, ancestral village, or Baltic or Black Sea beaches. Winters were grim, with long nights and short days, and little sun until February. Snowfall was not as bad as I had expected, but when it did snow, the removal crews, "manned" mostly by women, were very efficient. The winter weather was tolerable, if you dressed appropriately with good boots and a fur hat, but when the wind blew, you learned not to stay out too long. You also learned how to wash your car in the embassy garage when the temperature dropped far below freezing. If you neglected to completely dry the car, you could end up with doors and windows frozen shut, and a prisoner in your own vehicle.

Cultural attractions, however, were many. Music, theater, and dance were outstanding. The intelligentsia, for those Americans who had access to it, was stimulating, and Russian friendship, for those who experienced it, was everlasting. Americans who could converse in Russian had unlimited opportunities to learn more about Russia and its people. And a tour of duty in Moscow provided a solid base for future assignments at the Department of State dealing with US-Soviet relations.

To prepare for an assignment in Moscow, language competence in Russian was a firm requirement. A working knowledge of the language could be acquired during a nine-month intensive course at the State Department's Foreign Service Institute (FSI), but I presented a problem for the FSI teachers. With my competence in Polish, a related Slavic language, and the basic Russian I had acquired on my own, I was well along in my study of Russian. Accordingly, I was given a tutor, rather than being placed in a class with beginning students. And so, for nine months I sat in a room alone with Aleksandr Nikolayevich Vasiliev, a former Russian teacher at Yale University, for five hours each day, trying to talk in Russian about everything under the sun.

---

[5] The American and British Embassies are believed to be the only embassies in Moscow that strictly observed the official rate of exchange, when other embassies were buying rubles at five to the dollar in Western Europe.

The Russian language at first appears to be a formidable challenge. But it is an Indo-European language and has many similarities with the languages many of us learned in school, like Latin, German, and French. The vocabulary is rich, and verbs can be given various shades of meanings by adding different prefixes. Many words of cultural context are from the French, medical and technical from the German, and now business from American English. Sitting in a room with a teacher for months can pay dividends, but there is no substitute for immersion in a Russian environment. I recall how pleased I was one day in Moscow when I learned that I could converse by telephone in Russian without fear or hesitation.

Welcome to Moscow

My arrival in Moscow in June 1967 was greeted by a demonstration, not in my honor but as a protest by Arab students against the Six-Day War in which Israel defeated its Middle Eastern neighbors.

I had just arrived to begin a two-year tour and, it being a beautiful Saturday in June, I decided to take a walk around the city. A walk around Moscow always produced interesting sights, especially for a curious American, and on this one I encountered two Orthodox Jews returning from their Sabbath synagogue service, and engaged them in an interesting street-corner conversation on the status of Jews in the Soviet Union.

As I returned to the American Embassy I encountered a marching crowd, and being curious about everything Russian, I joined them and was swept along with the marchers as they approached the embassy. The Moscow *militsia* (police), intent on avoiding violence, had everything under control. The demonstrators were orderly as they chanted their slogans and hurled projectiles at the embassy, but there was no burning of American cars, as in other countries. Forewarned of the demonstration, all American cars had been removed from the streets around the embassy.

And so it came about that a newly arrived cultural officer had an insider's view of a staged anti-American demonstration, which surprised other embassy officers as they spied me among the demonstrators they were surveying and filming from the chancery's upper floors.

From that day, I made it a practice every day to take a break from reading telegrams, and to get out of the embassy for a walk around Moscow or to make a call on a Soviet institution, a practice that never failed to turn up something of interest in that city of secrecy and intrigue.

The Moscow Journalists' Club

The House of the Journalist (*Dom Zhurnalista*) was a segregated institution when I arrived in Moscow. Membership in the club was open to journalists of the Soviet Union and its communist allies but not to Western correspondents accredited in Moscow. But the doors opened a crack after I made my introductory call at the Press Department of the USSR Ministry of Foreign Affairs.

The Press Department was headed by Leonid Zamyatin, a journalist who had served several years as a correspondent in New York where he earned a reputation as a hardliner who faithfully followed the Moscow line and seemed to enjoy doing so. Zamyatin, moreover, was seen as a "comer" and had been mentioned as a future ambassador to Washington. I was new to the Soviet Union but determined not to let the Cold War get in the way of doing my job as I had done in previous postings as a cultural or press attaché.

"Normalization" was the US objective at the time—to normalize relations with the Soviet Union—and in my efforts to do so I attempted to normalize work conditions for American correspondents. My call at the Press Department, however, was considered routine since I was the embassy officer concerned with American correspondents, their relations with the Press Department, and the conditions under which they worked.

Working conditions for Western correspondents in Moscow were very restrictive in those years, and the list of complaints was long. Access to news sources was strictly controlled by the Soviet authorities. Interviews with government officials had to be requested through the Press Department, and were rarely given. Travel within the Soviet Union was severely limited.

Most of Soviet territory at that time was closed to Westerners—the Russian secrecy syndrome—and travel plans for foreign correspondents had to be filed with the Press Department forty-eight hours in advance, even to areas normally open to travel. That enabled the KGB to decide whether it wanted foreigners in those areas at a particular time, and to alert local authorities to their itineraries. Moreover, travel to normally open areas was often denied by the Ministry "for reasons of a temporary nature." In 1968, for example, Western correspondents and diplomats were denied permission over a period of several weeks to visit Leningrad, although embassy telephone inquiries to American students there failed to disclose any unusual events in the Soviet Union's second largest city, which at that time did not have an American Consulate.

It was also difficult in those years for American correspondents to get into the Soviet Union, and sometimes equally difficult to get out. An informal agreement between the two governments limited the number of correspondents in each other's country, and in 1967 the number for each side was twenty-six. Accredited correspondents were issued single-entry visas, and they and their family members had to request exit visas in order to leave the Soviet Union. That caused delays when correspondents were asked by their home offices to cover an event in a neighboring country, or when family illness required prompt medical evacuation to Western Europe where quality care was available. And it was not unusual for Westerners to be harassed by the KGB—sometimes violently—and even expelled for showing too much zeal in ferreting out news in a secrecy-obsessed society.

American diplomats, as well as correspondents, traveled in pairs in those years—the safety in numbers theory—and that included calls by diplomats at the Ministry of Foreign Affairs where one American spoke and the other took notes. So when I entered Zamyatin's office at the Ministry unaccompanied, he appeared surprised and immediately summoned his two deputies. The Soviets, apparently, also had a safety in numbers practice. The three Soviet officials evidenced obvious curiosity about this new American diplomat who had ventured a solitary foray into their Ministry.

After introductory pleasantries, I opened with my line of feigned innocence—Russians and Americans should work together to normalize relations between our two countries, including normal working conditions for American correspondents in Moscow. I pointed out that Soviet correspondents in Washington could attend press briefings by US government officials and were accorded one-on-one interviews. Zamyatin countered sharply that he had been continually harassed by the FBI during his years as a correspondent in New York, and his rejoinder set the tone for the remainder of our conversation. With charge and countercharge, recriminations piled up on both sides as my hopes for normalization receded.

Near the close of our strained conversation I reminded Zamyatin that he and his fellow Soviet correspondents in the United States were accorded membership privileges in the National Press Club in Washington and the Overseas Press Club in New York. By contrast, I continued, Americans in Moscow were denied entry to the Dom Zhurnalista, the Moscow press club. Membership in the club would have enabled Western correspondents to socialize with Soviet journalists and perhaps learn more about what was going on in that closed society. But the club also boasted one of the better restaurants in Moscow, at a time when food and service were not very satisfying in most Russian restaurants. Zamyatin was noncommittal about press club membership, and I took my leave wondering what my visit had accomplished. So much for normalization, I thought.

One month later, however, I received in the mail a plain envelope with no return address, containing a card in my name, authorizing entry to the Dom Zhurnalista on Thursday evenings. Thursday was film night at the club, and after a good dinner in the club restaurant, visitors could see the best of Soviet and foreign films, including many that were never released to the Soviet public. A quick check revealed that all American correspondents accredited in Moscow had received similar cards. My approach had worked. The Dom Zhurnalista had been integrated, at least on Thursday evenings.

During the next few months I was an occasional visitor to the club on Thursdays. The food was good, the films revealing, and it was often possible to strike up an interesting conversation with a Soviet journalist. On one visit, however, the conversation was more interesting than anticipated.

On that evening I entered the club, checked my coat, and was greeted by a white-jacketed waiter who, recognizing me as a foreigner, bowed low and requested that I follow him. I did and found myself in a private dining room filled with prominent Soviet journalists and officials, seated at tables, enjoying their food and drink, and obviously celebrating some kind of event. The celebration, I learned, was the fiftieth anniversary of the founding of TASS, the Soviet news agency. Realizing that the waiter had erred and that American diplomats had not been invited to the TASS birthday party, I expressed my apologies and turned to leave.

Russian hospitality, however, would not allow that, and I was invited to take a seat and join in the festivities. And so I found myself sitting next to a distinguished-looking, grey-haired Soviet Army officer with general's insignia on his shoulder boards. We introduced ourselves and he turned out to be Lt. General Nikolai I. Makeyev, the long-time editor of *Krasnaya zvezda* (Red Star), the Soviet Army daily.

Thus it came about that, at the height of the Vietnam War, an American diplomat had dinner with a Soviet general. We discussed our work, the state of relations between our two countries, and raised our vodka glasses far too many times to "*mir i druzhba*" (peace and friendship) between our two countries. *Omnia pro patria*!

General Makeyev remained at *Krasnaya zvezda* until 1985, when he was removed by Mikhail Gorbachev after thirty years as chief editor. Leonid Zamyatin was passed over for the position of ambassador to Washington but made it to London as ambassador, also in 1985. In August 1991, however, when news of the attempted coup against Gorbachev reached London, Zamyatin supported it, and two days later he was recalled to Moscow. The old Journalists' Club, however, is still there, only now its restaurant and café have been privatized and are open to anyone who can pay the prices. And the food is still rather good.

The integration of the Moscow Journalists' Club was one small step in opening up a closed society, a process that many younger Russian authorities recognized as necessary but thought they could control. But it took another eighteen years, and many more small steps under Mikhail Gorbachev, before Soviet society really opened up. By then, however, Russians had been given too many freedoms, control was no longer possible, and communism collapsed.

Copyright or Wrong?

In autumn 1967, as the newly arrived Counselor for Press and Culture, I embarked on a series of calls on various Soviet ministries and organizations involved in cultural exchanges, including some where no American diplomat had previously ventured. I was determined to do what I had done in other posts, and not be cowed by Soviet restrictions. I was never refused a visit, and was always received correctly, if not cordially.

At the Union of Composers, I met with Tikhon Khrennikov, the conservative composer who, at the behest of Stalin, had so tormented Dmitri Shostakovich and Sergei Prokofiev. And at the Gorky Institute of World Literature, from where writers Andrei Sinyavsky and Yuli Daniel had been imprisoned the previous year for publishing "anti-Soviet" works, I established contact with scholars in the American section. A few months later, I surprised them with an invitation to an embassy showing of the classic film, *Gone With the Wind.* Two of them came, with their wives, and enjoyed the film that told them much about the antebellum South they had been writing about.

At the Union of Soviet Writers, we discussed exchanges of writers, which were already taking place under the cultural agreement, but the conversation eventually got around to copyright protection and the Soviet practice of publishing American authors without compensation. The USSR in those years was not a party to an international copyright convention, and I pointed out that by not doing so it was losing hard currency, because American publishers were also free to publish Soviet authors without compensation. To prove my point, I offered to provide the Writers' Union with a list of Soviet books recently published in the United States if, in exchange, the Union would give me a list of American books published in the Soviet Union.

We shook hands on that, and a few months later, with the cooperation of the Association of American Publishers, USIA sent me a list of Soviet books published in the United States, which I presented to the Union of Writers. And, a month or so later, the Union presented me with a list of American authors published in the Soviet Union. Both lists were longer than I had expected, and included many scientific as well as literary works.

I don't know whether that exchange of lists persuaded the Soviet Union to accede to the Universal Copyright Convention (UCC) in 1973, but it may have helped to tip the balance in favor of Soviet writers who had been seeking protection for their works published abroad.

Romney and Arbatov—A Tale of Two Georges

George Romney came to Moscow in December 1967 during the early months of his campaign for the Republican nomination for US president. The former head of American Motors and three-term governor of Michigan was clearly presidential timber. He was tall, handsome, articulate, intelligent, and a successful businessman, but his experience had been mostly in domestic politics, and he needed some foreign exposure to enhance his bid for the presidency. To give him some international seasoning, a whirlwind twenty-eight-day, round-the-world trip was undertaken.

American politicians, it used to be said, had to visit the three I's—Ireland, Italy, and Israel to be elected to public office. Russia was added to that list when Romney stopped in Moscow for three days, thus becoming the first declared US presidential candidate to visit Russia. Many others would follow in subsequent campaigns.

Romney's advance party arrived in Moscow in early December to make plans for his visit later that month. In a meeting at the American Embassy, they asked if their man could meet with a group of average Soviet citizens, a request not unusual for an American politician. But the Vietnam War was escalating, US-Soviet relations were not good, and it was questionable whether Soviet authorities would give their approval. As the embassy's Counselor for Press and Cultural Affairs, I replied that the Soviets could certainly arrange such a meeting if they wished, but I warned not to expect average citizens. But since the American ambassador could not play partisan politics by hosting a meeting for a candidate for US political office, who then could do it?

Moscow at that time had an Institute for Soviet-American Relations, a "quango" (quasi non-governmental organization), affiliated with the network of Soviet friendship societies that conducted cultural exchanges with other countries. Staffed with personnel who had served in the United States, the institute was knowledgeable about America and well qualified to host the meeting if higher-ups gave the go-ahead. But the American embassy did not have official contact with the Institute, regarding it as a Soviet effort to end run the intergovernmental exchange agreement. However, in a meeting with Ambassador Thompson, I argued that the Institute could be useful to us, and it was time to recognize its existence. Thompson concurred, and when the Romney advance party met with Institute officials, they readily agreed to host the proposed meeting with "average" Soviet citizens that was to take place in Friendship House (*Dom Druzhbi*), home of the Soviet friendship societies.

After arriving in Moscow on 18 December, Romney was briefed by Ambassador Thompson and visited the Moscow automobile factory where, as a successful Detroit auto tycoon, he kicked a few tires and talked shop with his communist counterparts. (If there was one type of American that Russian communists respected, it was the successful capitalist.) Romney also had several photo ops, including a pre-dawn jog in Red Square with embassy Marine guards.

The highlight of the Romney visit was a meeting with Soviet Premier Aleksei Kosygin in the Kremlin where they discussed Vietnam, arms control, the Arab-Israeli conflict, and US-Soviet relations. The Kosygin meeting was a surprise because the war in Vietnam was raging, and earlier that year Soviet officials had refused to meet with former Vice President Nixon when he had visited Moscow. Romney, however, opposed the war and was publicly espousing a neutralization of Vietnam.

Romney's meeting with average Soviet citizens was scheduled for 4 P.M. following a sightseeing tour of the Kremlin. Thirty minutes before the meeting was scheduled to start, I received a call from Dmitri Muravyev, Secretary General of the Institute for Soviet-American Relations, who requested that the meeting be postponed because he could not round up enough Soviet citizens. There were no cell phones in those days, so I explained that Romney was out sightseeing and could not be reached, and I urged the Institute to continue its efforts to find more citizens.

Twenty minutes later, only ten minutes before the scheduled start, Muravyev called again, frantic this time, and said that the meeting *must* be postponed because he simply could not get enough Soviet citizens to attend. I suggested that he call the Ministry of Foreign Affairs, *Pravda,* and TASS, adding that they must have people there who would welcome the opportunity to meet a man who might be the next American president. I even suggested that the Institute had the wherewithal to round up some citizens from Moscow streets, if necessary. Concluding the conversation, I said that I would be at Friendship House in ten minutes as earlier agreed.

At 4 P.M. I was at the curb in front of Friendship House as Romney pulled up in the Ambassador's Cadillac, unaware of any hitch in the planned event. Opening the car door, I escorted him into the building where, to my surprise, some fifty of the most prominent Moscow citizens were assembled—scholars, scientists, journalists, and government officials. Waiters were standing by with trays of vodka and *zakuski* (Russian hors d'oeuvres), and the meeting commenced with no indication, or explanation, of the reported difficulties in rounding up average citizens.

At the reception I was introduced to a Russian, Georgy Arbatov, whose name was new to the embassy. When asked what he did, Arbatov replied that he had just been named to head a new Institute for USA Studies (Canada was to be added later), also unknown at the time. When asked about his qualifications for the job and whether he had ever visited the United States, Arbatov replied with one of his clever one-liners. "I am neutral on the United States," he said with a smile, "because I have never been there, and that is why I have been chosen for the job."

Romney departed Moscow for Israel and other stops on his round-the-world trip, but his bid for the Republican nomination was not successful. Richard Nixon was eventually received by Soviet officials but only after he had become president and initiated détente, a new chapter in US-Soviet relations.

Arbatov's career in international affairs, however, was just beginning, and in the following months I met with him several times to discuss his initial US visit, scheduled for September 1968. Arbatov wanted the American Embassy to expedite his US visa and facilitate his meetings in Washington. The visit was delayed, however, by one of those unforeseen events that, from time to time, have set back US-Soviet relations—this time, the Soviet invasion of Czechoslovakia in August 1968.

Acting on instructions from the State Department, it fell to me to inform Arbatov that his visit to the United States so soon after the invasion "would not be productive," meaning that he would not be received by US officials. His long-awaited American debut had to be put off until after the inauguration of Richard Nixon as president.

Arbatov eventually made his American debut in 1969, seven months later than originally planned. On that visit, in a call at the State Department, Arbatov kept his US host, Department Soviet specialist Boris Klosson, waiting for ten minutes, most likely by plan, and in receiving Arbatov, Klosson noted that he was ten minutes late.

"No," replied Arbatov with another of his one-liners, "I am seven months and ten minutes late."

Winston Churchill once described Russia as "a riddle, wrapped in a mystery, inside an enigma," and for many years I wondered what had caused the attempted postponement of Romney's Friendship House meeting at almost the last minute. The answer to that riddle came in 1991 during a chance encounter I had in Moscow with a Russian official who had helped to plan the Romney visit.

Shortly before the Romney meeting at Friendship House was to start, I was told, his Soviet hosts realized that they had failed to request authorization from higher-ups in the Party. A call to the Central Committee revealed that there was no objection to the meeting, but no one there was willing to give the authorization without going still higher in the Party hierarchy.

The Party official whose authorization was needed was Mikhail Suslov, the Politburo member in charge of ideology, but no one at the Central Committee staff had the courage to call such a high and mighty figure. When someone was finally found who dared to call Suslov, he readily gave his approval, only minutes before the scheduled start.

George Romney did not make it to the White House but Georgy Arbatov continued to head the Institute for US and Canadian Studies for many years, serving as an apologist abroad for a succession of Moscow leaders from Brezhnev to Gorbachev and Yeltsin.

Cultural Exchange

US-Soviet cultural exchange with the West—and with the United States in particular—conducted over a period of thirty years, helped to prepare the way for the end of the Cold War, and at a fraction of the cost of our military and intelligence operations over the same years. It's a little-known story that needs to be told.[6]

---

[6] For details of the effectiveness of US-Soviet cultural exchanges, see Richmond, *Cultural Exchange and the Cold War*. The book also covers in detail the scholarly exchanges conducted under the US-Soviet cultural agreement.

Stalin's Iron Curtain was real and almost insurmountable. As a result, Soviet knowledge of the West was abysmal, and US knowledge of the Soviet Union was not much better. And it was not only Russia's common people who were so ignorant of the world beyond Soviet borders, but also Russia's intellectuals. When Oxford scholar Isaiah Berlin, in 1956, was able to meet with Boris Pasternak and Anna Akhmatova, two of Russia's leading writers, he wrote: "I told [them] all that I could of English, American, French writing: it was like speaking to the victims of shipwreck on a desert island, cut off for decades from civilization—all they heard, they received as new, exciting and delightful."[7]

After Stalin's death in 1953, cracks began to appear in the previously impenetrable Iron Curtain. An American company of *Porgy and Bess,* on tour in Europe in 1955, was invited by the Soviets to perform in Leningrad and Moscow, where they were a smash hit. Similar successes were enjoyed the following year by the Boston Symphony, violinist Isaac Stern, and tenor Jan Peerce (who sang Yiddish songs as encores). Cracks in the Iron Curtain widened when Nikita Khrushchev, at the Twentieth Congress of the Soviet Communist Party in February 1956, attacked Stalin and called for increased contacts with the West.

In that same month a group of American scholars established the Inter-University Committee on Travel Grants (IUCTG), to administer, with Ford Foundation funding, thirty-day visits for American students and professors traveling as tourists, the only way they could visit the Soviet Union at the time.[8]

One year later, in summer 1957, the Soviets staged in Moscow their Sixth World Youth Festival, a propaganda extravaganza intended to show the changes since Stalin's death. But the results were quite different, and the consequences unintended. The tens of thousands of Soviet youth who saw the show were infected with the youth styles of the Western attendees—jeans,

---

[7] Cited in Mayers, *The Ambassadors,* 197.

[8] With the signature of the first US-Soviet cultural agreement in 1958, IUCTG also administered the exchanges of US and Soviet graduate students, senior scholars, and language teachers conducted under the agreement. In 1968, IUCTG was succeeded by IREX (International Research and Exchanges Board) as US administrator of those exchanges. For more on scholarly exchanges, see Robert F. Byrnes, *Soviet-American Academic Exchanges, 1958–1975* (Bloomington, IN: Indiana University Press, 1976).

jazz, boogie woogie, rock and roll, and free speech—and the Soviet Union would never again be the same.

"The government's inability to regulate the musical fare at the Sixth World Youth Festival," wrote rock historian Timothy W. Ryback, "... highlighted the cultural dilemma that plagued Soviet officials for the next decade. With jazz ensembles thriving in every city ... officials found it impossible to control the wave of Western music sweeping the Soviet republics."[9]

Along with the jazz groups from Western Europe, also to Moscow came some of the early rock and roll groups from Britain with their electric guitars, that were new to the Soviet Union. Rock was unknown in Moscow, and it took the festival by storm. Despite later efforts to stem the tide, rock continued to roll on, and with devastating consequences for Soviet ideologists.

The influence of the Beatles on western youth is well known. Less well known is their following among Soviet youth, and the changes they wrought. "We knew their songs by heart," writes Pavel Palazchenko, Gorbachev's English-language interpreter and foreign policy aide, "they helped us create a world of our own, a world different from the dull and senseless ideological liturgy that increasingly reminded one of Stalinism ... the Beatles were our quiet way of rejecting 'the system' while conforming to most of its demands."[10]

Rock taught Russians to speak more freely, to express their innermost thoughts, as singers Vysotsky and Okudzhava, and poets Voznesensky and Yevtushenko, had done a generation earlier. And rock therefore has to be seen as another reason for the collapse of communism.

That is not as farfetched as it may seem. It is a claim made by many Russians, and also by Andras Simonyi, the current Hungarian ambassador to the United States, who led a rock band in Budapest during the Cold War. In an address titled, "How Rock Music Helped Bring Down the Iron Curtain," Simonyi said, "Rock 'n 'roll, culturally speaking, was a decisive

---

[9] Timothy W. Ryback, *Rock Around the Bloc: A History of Rock Music in Eastern Europe and the Soviet Union* (New York: Oxford University Press, 1990), 30.

[10] Pavel Palazchenko, *My Years with Gorbachev and Shevardnadze: The Memoir of a Soviet Interpreter* (University Park, PA: Pennsylvania State University Press, 1997), 3.

element in loosening up communist societies and bring them closer to the world of freedom."[11]

The Beatles never played in Moscow, but when Elton John performed there in 1979, he was asked to delete the Beatles' song, "Back in the USSR," from his repertoire. The best tickets had been distributed to party functionaries and their families, and the show was received coolly by the audience until the encore, when Elton John played the banned song and almost caused a riot.

The Rolling Stones, in their heyday, also never made it to Moscow, but when they were finally allowed to perform there in 1998, they filled a sports stadium with fifty thousand cheering Russians, many of them in their thirties and forties, who had waited more than twenty years to hear and see them live on stage.

The Beatles also had fans at the highest levels of the Soviet government. In 1987, Mikhail Gorbachev and his wife Raisa told Yoko Ono, John Lennon's widow, that they were Beatles fans. That endorsement ended three decades of official Soviet anti-rock policy.

Tours by Soviet artists across the United States under the US-USSR cultural agreement were also an eye opener. "America was for us simply another planet," said Bolshoi ballerina Galina Ulanova after her first visit in 1959. "We knew so little about the outside world, and we were just amazed by the scale of the country. All those huge stores five and six floors high, with all these clothes on sale, and entire apartments on display—we just didn't have anything like that."[12]

Equally impressed was choreographer Igor Moiseyev: "I'm amazed that all your workers are fat and all your millionaires are thin."[13] It was exactly the opposite of what he had been led to believe from caricatures of Americans in Soviet political cartoons.

For Soviet artists and audiences, isolated from the West since the 1930s, the visits to the Soviet Union by American and

---

[11] Bill Nichols, "How Rock 'n' Roll Freed the World," *USA Today,* 6 November 2003.

[12] Galina Ulanova, in Harlow Robinson, *The Last Impresario: The Life, Times, and Legacy of Sol Hurok* (New York: Viking, 1994), 376.

[13] Igor Moiseyev, in Robinson, *The Last Impresario,* 355.

other Western performers brought fresh air as well as new artistic concepts in music, dance, and theater to a country where orthodoxy and conservatism had long been guiding principles in the arts.

When George Balanchine took his New York City Ballet to Leningrad in 1962, the reception was revolutionary. As Solomon Volkov, a Russian cultural historian, wrote: "The young saw in Balanchine's productions the heights that the Petersburg cultural avant-garde could have reached if it had not been crushed by the Soviet authorities."[14]

In theater, the sixteen performances in Moscow and Leningrad of Thornton Wilder's *Our Town* and Lawrence and Lee's *Inherit the Wind* by Washington's Arena Stage in 1973 enjoyed similar success. Performances were sold out weeks in advance, and thousands of ticket seekers had to be turned away. *Our Town* touched on human experiences common to Russians and Americans, and one Soviet cultural official likened Wilder to Anton Chekhov. The cheering audiences, rave press reviews, and offstage rapport with the visiting Americans all made for a very satisfying experience. On her return to Washington, Arena artistic director Zelda Fichandler summed up the trip:

> There was widespread astonishment that the kind of theater represented by Arena Stage even existed in America. They had always thought of American theater as being made up of musical comedies, Broadway hits produced by pick-up companies with the aim of making profits, and what they called 'sexual clownery.' ...We were, as one Soviet writer put it, 'something totally unexpected.'[15]

Inherit the Wind reenacted the "monkey trial" of 1925 in which John Scopes, a Tennessee teacher, was charged with teaching evolution to his students. Soviet ideologists saw the play as a struggle between religion and science in which religion won, but the play was also about freedom of speech, and the message of a state imposing its ideology was not lost on the Soviet audience, which heard it through simultaneous translation. *Inherit* was performed while Aleksandr Solzhenitsyn and Andrei Sakharov were being harassed in the Soviet Union for their views.

---

[14] Solomon Volkov, *New York Times,* 9 September 2001, trans. Antonina W. Bouis.
[15] Zelda Fichandler, in address to National Press Club, Washington, D.C., 26 November 1973.

Another opening to the West was provided by US jazz greats who came to the Soviet Union under the cultural agreement: Benny Goodman, Woody Herman, Earl Hines, Duke Ellington, Preservation Hall Jazz Band, New York Jazz Repertory, Dave Brubeck, and the Thad Jones-Mel Lewis Orchestra. For Ellington's 1971 Moscow performances, tickets were sold on the black market for as much as eighty rubles, when the usual price for a theater ticket was seldom higher than four rubles.

But did such cultural exchanges really change the Soviet Union? One answer is given by a Russian musician. "We were raised," he explained, "on propaganda that portrayed Soviet society as the wave of the future, while the West was decadent and doomed. And yet," he continued, "From that 'decadent' West, there came to the Soviet Union great symphony orchestras with electrifying sounds, and they came year after year, from Boston, Philadelphia, New York, Cleveland, and San Francisco. How could the decadent West produce such great orchestras," we asked ourselves. "Cultural exchanges were another opening to the West, and additional proof that our media were not telling us the truth.[16]

Exchanges of American and Soviet writers were also influential in bringing change. Of his one-month visit to the Soviet Union, American writer Ted Solotaroff wrote:

> What Russian writers got out of visiting American writers was, to them, our spectacular freedom to speak our minds. There we were, official representatives of the US … who had no party line at all, in most cases, except the party of humanity, and who had the writer's tendency to speak out on controversial issues. I did so often in the month I was there, and each time I could see how much I was envied … the exchanges enabled Soviet writers, intellectuals, and students to see that the "Free World" wasn't just political cant.[17]

The meaning of such meetings to Soviet writers was shown by what Soviet poets privately told American poet Stanley Kunitz, at a US-Soviet writers' meeting at a Black Sea resort in 1979. "Bear with us," they said, "Eventually, the old hardliners will die off. Time is on our side. Keep coming."[18] Time was

---

[16] Miron Yampolsky, author's interview, Reston, VA, 4 August 1999.

[17] Ted Solotaroff, e-mail to author, 17 September 2000.

[18] Stanley Kunitz, quoted by Herbert Mitgang in "Book Ends," *New York Times Book Review*, 23 December 1979.

indeed on their side, and the Americans kept coming, well into the 1980s when change had come to the Soviet Union.

Cultural exchange can also combat anti-Americanism. As George F. Kennan, America's premier diplomat, put it:

> I personally attach ... high importance to cultural contact as a means of combating the negative impressions about this country that mark so much of world opinion. What we have to do ... is to show the outside world both that we have a cultural life and that we care something about it—that we care enough about it ... to give it encouragement and support here at home, and to see that it is enriched by acquaintance with similar activity elsewhere. If these impressions could only be conveyed with enough force and success to countries beyond our borders, I for my part would willingly trade the entire remaining inventory of political propaganda for the results that could be achieved by such means alone.[19]

Goskontsert

The USSR State Concert Agency, *Goskontsert*, was the impresario of the Soviet Union, sending its performing artists abroad and receiving foreign artists in the Soviet Union. It was the government monopoly we had to deal with in implementing performing arts exchanges under the US-Soviet cultural agreement. And like all Soviet government agencies, it was a model of inefficiency and delay, but also capable of decision and dispatch when necessity demanded.

Soviet performing artists—symphony orchestras, ballet troupes, individual artists, as well as circuses and ice shows— were good box office attractions in the United States, and big dollar earners for the Soviet state. Moreover, Goskontsert was free to shop among competing American concert agencies for the most favorable terms. Americans, however, had to deal with a state monopoly governed by Soviet ideology.

The cultural agreement specified how many performing arts groups and individual artists would be exchanged over two or three years, but the limit on individual artists was seldom enforced. In addition, the artists to be exchanged needed the approval of both parties to the agreement. The United States exercised its veto several times when the State Department,

---

[19] George F. Kennan, in address at a symposium sponsored by the International Council of The Museum of Modern Art, New York, 12 May 1955.

fearing protests by émigré groups after the Soviet suppression of the 1956 Hungarian revolution, said that it would not grant visas for tours by the Soviet Army Chorus. Goskontsert, for its part, reflecting the basic conservatism of Russian communist officials and ideologists, rejected many of the modern dance groups and jazz ensembles proposed by the State Department. I can recall several meetings with Goskontsert deputy director Golovin in which he described American ensembles we were proposing as "too avant garde." And until the late 1980s, rock music was out of the question.

Financial arrangements for the two sides also differed. Tours by Soviet artists in the United States were contracted directly with US impresarios, and proceeds from their performances went, not to the artists but to the Soviet embassy in Washington. The Soviets usually delivered their artists to the United States via Aeroflot, and US impresarios paid for all local costs, including hotels, domestic travel, meals, and modest stipends. Financial gains for the Soviet state were believed to have been considerable. One informed estimate in 1978 put the yearly earnings between $300,000 and $1,000,000.[20]

The State Department likewise delivered American artists to the Soviet Union where their local costs were covered by Goskontsert. However, US performing arts groups going to the Soviet Union were paid a fee in dollars by the State Department, and proceeds from their performances in the Soviet Union were paid to the American Embassy in Russian rubles, which the embassy used to cover some of its local expenses in Moscow.

The transfer of such rubles was an ordeal. Goskontsert had no system for writing checks, and embassy cultural officers had to go to its offices with empty suitcases for the stacks of rubles that were carefully counted out by hand.

"S. Hurok Presents"

Tours of Soviet performing artists in the United States could not take place without the assistance of US concert agencies,

---

[20] See Boris H. Klosson, "Survey of US Educational and Cultural Exchanges with the Soviet Union and Eastern Europe," p.112, a classified report prepared by Klosson for the Department of State on 23 June 1978, and declassified under the Freedom of Information Act on 24 December 1984.

and among the impresarios who worked with the Soviets, Sol Hurok was a pioneer. In the early years of the exchanges, his Hurok Concerts Inc. brought to the United States many of the leading Soviet artists and artistic ensembles, such as the Bolshoi and Kirov Ballets, and the Moiseyev Folk Dance Ensemble, which would become staples in Soviet-American exchanges and did much to encourage ballet and folk dancing in the United States.

In a highly competitive business, Hurok had several advantages over his US rivals. He had the unfailing nose of a good impresario in judging what would fill concert halls, and he had experience in the concert agency business dating back to 1913. But equally important, Hurok understood the Russians and spoke their language, an undeniable advantage in dealing with them. Born in Ukraine, he had emigrated to the United States in 1906 at the age of eighteen.

Hurok's visits to Moscow were always events to be remembered. His arrival would be announced in advance to the American Embassy by a State Department telegram, which gave his flight number and indicated that he expected to be met at the airport by an embassy officer.

As embassy Counselor for Cultural Affairs, I was faced with a dilemma the first time I received such a message. An airport "meet" could take three hours out of a busy day, and if I met Hurok the first time, I would have to meet him on subsequent visits to Moscow. I decided to risk his disappointment and not meet him. He would be met, in any event, by Goskontsert, provided with a Soviet car and driver during his Moscow stay, and that would have to suffice.

A call on the American ambassador was routine for Hurok, to get a briefing on the current state of US-Soviet relations and to determine the political atmosphere in Moscow, always an important factor in cultural exchanges. Hurok also expected an invitation to lunch with the ambassador or, at the least, drinks at the residence.

On one occasion, Hurok was invited for cocktails by Ambassador and Mrs. Beam, along with Agnes de Mille, the famed American dancer and choreographer, who happened to be in Moscow at the time. It was an evening I'll never forget, as the two of them, who had known each other for many years, traded barbs as well as anecdotes. The Beams may not have known that Hurok and de Mille had tangled many times since

1929 when Hurok refused her proposal that he manage her.[21] Moreover, de Mille's husband, Walter Prude, was an employee of Hurok, and provided the polish that Hurok lacked. But when Hurok died in 1975, at the age of eighty-five, he failed to acknowledge, in any way, Prude's twenty-eight years of loyal and productive service.[22]

Hurok, although not physically imposing, was not known to underestimate his importance, and he attracted attention wherever he went. A broad brimmed fedora and a silver-handled walking stick were his trademarks, and in later life he sported pastel-colored dress shirts when most men were still wearing white.

He was usually put up by the Soviets in Suite 107 in Moscow's venerable National Hotel, overlooking the Kremlin and Red Square. When I once called on him there, I remarked that Suite 107 had been Lenin's. "No," he replied with a condescending smile, "this is Hurok's suite."

Calling on him one afternoon at "Hurok's suite," I found him seated at a table in the living room drinking tea with several elderly Russian women, whom he introduced to me as his Moscow relatives. It looked like a scene out of New York's old Bronx.

Yekaterina Furtseva was Soviet Minister of Culture during the 1970s, the détente years when US-Soviet exchanges greatly expanded, and she and Hurok had a good working relationship. Both had roots in Ukraine, Furtseva as the daughter of a peasant family, and Hurok as a Jew playing the traditional role of middleman in an agricultural society.

Hurok treated Furtseva with great respect, which she appreciated, and in his conversations with me, he always referred to her as "the lady." Although the Soviets were adept at playing off one US impresario against another, Hurok nevertheless had a favored position. The Soviets could count on him to do favors for them, as he did when "S. Hurok Presents" brought the Bolshoi Opera to the United States in 1975, one year after Hurok's death, although it was known that while it would be a box office success, it would also be a big money-loser because of the size of its company.

---

[21] Carol Easton, *No Intermissions: The Life of Agnes de Mille* (Boston: Little, Brown and Company, 1996), 331.

[22] Ibid., 438.

Hurok's objectives in visiting Moscow were to see what the Soviets had to offer in the performing arts, to keep his channels open, and to strike a deal. When I asked him, at the conclusion of one of his Moscow visits, whether he had signed any contracts, he replied boastfully that he did not need to sign contracts with the Soviets. A handshake and his word sufficed, he said, and if the Soviets wanted something on paper, he would write out the terms himself on a scrap of paper.[23]

Hurok was the last of a generation of great impresarios, and a colorful personality who made a difference.

Thematic Exhibitions

"Better to see once than hear a hundred times," advises an old Russian proverb, and Russians heeded that advice in flocking to see the twenty-three thematic exhibitions produced by USIA under the cultural agreement. What they had heard a hundred times about the United States from their own media was negated by a single visit to one of the USIA touring exhibitions, which gave them a glimpse of the United States, its people, and how they lived. The exhibitions, which were shown between 1959 and 1991, also provided a rare opportunity for Soviet citizens to talk with Russian-speaking American guides and ask questions about the United States.

The cultural agreement provided for month-long showings of exhibitions in three cities (later increased to six, and then nine) over the two (later three) years of each agreement, to portray life in the two countries and the latest developments in a number of specialized fields. Among the themes of the US exhibitions were medicine, technical books, graphic arts, architecture, hand tools, education, research and development, outdoor recreation, technology for the home, photography, agriculture, information, and industrial design. The US exhibitions drew huge crowds, with lines stretching for blocks awaiting admittance, and were seen, on average, by some 250,000 visitors in each city. All told, more than twenty million Soviet citizens are believed to have seen the twenty-three exhibitions

---

[23] Years later, a former Hurok staffer told me that those Moscow visits, which resulted in oral agreements but no written contracts, created great difficulties for his New York office which then had to laboriously negotiate the contract terms with Goskontsert.

over the thirty-two–year period.[24] It was Public Diplomacy on a massive scale.

The exchange began in 1959 with US and Soviet national exhibitions at Moscow's Sokolniki Park and New York City's Coliseum. That exchange received wide publicity because it was at Sokolniki that then Vice-President Richard Nixon and Soviet Premier Nikita Khrushchev, while touring a model American home, engaged in what has come to be known as the "kitchen debate."[25]

A special attraction of that and subsequent US exhibitions were the twenty or more young Russian-speaking American guides who explained the various items on display and fielded questions from the Soviet visitors. The conversations were spirited and open despite attempts, at times, by Komsomol provocateurs to disrupt them. For most of the Soviet visitors, it was their first and only opportunity to speak with an American.

Many of the American guides would go on to make careers in the Soviet area as scholars, professors, diplomats, and journalists. With their first-hand knowledge of life in the Soviet provinces, they became a national asset during the Cold War years when US knowledge of the Soviet Union was minimal. American visitors to the Soviet Union in those years usually traveled no further than Moscow, Leningrad, and Kiev, but the exhibitions and their guides also went to places seldom visited by foreigners in those years, such as Volgograd, Alma Ata, Baku, Tashkent, Ufa, Zaporozhye, Tselinograd, Rostov, and Novosibirsk.

Soviet visitors to the exhibitions were mostly male and in the early- to mid-twenties age group. They asked a variety of questions about life in the United States and listened to the guides' responses with great interest and openmindedness. Statements entered by visitors in the comment books were largely favorable. Many questions were also asked about international issues and world affairs, but that depended to some extent on the city—more in Moscow, Leningrad, and Kiev, and less in provincial cities—and the degree to which local authorities harassed visitors or sought to limit attendance.

---

[24] These statistics are from the file, "Special International Exhibitions," in the Historical Collection, Bureau of Public Diplomacy, Department of State, Washington, D.C.

[25] For a first-hand account of the kitchen debate, see the Letter to the Editor by Hans N. Tuch in the *Washington Post,* 31 August 1987.

Amerika Magazine

One result of the four-power Geneva Foreign Ministers Conference in 1955, only two years after the death of Stalin, was a US-Soviet agreement the following year for the reciprocal distribution of illustrated monthly magazines about life in the two countries, *Amerika* (*America Illustrated*) in Russian in the Soviet Union, and *USSR* (later renamed *Soviet Life*) in English in the United States.

An earlier version of *Amerika* had been distributed in the Soviet Union from 1945 to 1952. Published bimonthly by the Office of War Information, it was so popular with Soviet readers that it was reluctantly discontinued by the US side after the return of "unsold" copies escalated and it became clear that the Soviet Union was not honoring its agreement on distribution. The signature of a new agreement in 1956, negotiated by Wallace W. Littell, the first USIA officer assigned to Moscow, provided for distribution of a later version of the magazine.

The new *Amerika,* published by USIA, was a prestige product. A sixty-page, large-format, glossy, Russian-language monthly with lots of color photos but no advertising, it was full of articles portraying life in the United States. Designed to use the best US journalistic practices in telling America's story to the Soviet people, the articles were acquired initially from *Life, Look, Fortune,* and other US magazines but later augmented with articles by freelance writers and Amerika's Washington staff.

The agreement provided for each side to sell 50,000 copies of its magazine monthly—a pittance in consideration of the size of the Soviet market and the demand for information about the United States—5,000 to be distributed through subscriptions, and the remaining 45,000 sold at newsstands in more than eighty cities. Each side was also authorized to distribute gratis through its embassy an additional 2,000 copies, later increased to 5,000. Like the exhibitions, it was Public Diplomacy with a mass audience.

The first issue of the new *Amerika* appeared in October 1956, even before signature of the cultural agreement. Although written for a mass audience, its graphics and text descriptions of life in the United States appealed to Soviet citizens at all levels of society. Particularly popular was its coverage of how Americans lived, worked, and played, from their kitchens to their workplaces and cars. Moreover, its photo treatment and editorial style were new to the Soviet print media and served as models for similar Soviet photo magazines

Due to its popular appeal, *Amerika* proved far more successful than *Soviet Life* since, with the exception of the communist *Daily Worker,* it was the only US publication on sale in the Soviet Union. By contrast, *Soviet Life* had to compete with a wide variety of US and foreign publications in a free market, and its contents were not always of interest to American readers. *Amerika* soon became a collector's item, and many Russians, even today, prize the issues they saved over the years.

To counter the popularity of *Amerika* and limit its distribution, the Soviet distributor again began to return "unsold" copies to the American Embassy, and it became obvious that the Soviets, in a gross distortion of reciprocity, were limiting sales of *Amerika* to the level of sales of *Soviet Life.* To further limit the effect of *Amerika* on the Soviet public, the Department of Propaganda and Agitation of the Communist Party's Central Committee issued a top secret directive.[26]

Party units were advised to encourage subscriptions to *Amerika* for "politically literate and ideologically stable people," Soviet bureaucratese for people who could be trusted. It was further advised that subscriptions should be entered, not in the usual manner at Soviet post offices but rather through "social organizations" at work enterprises and institutions, which also ensured party control. Regarding retail sales, the Central Committee recommended that the magazine be sold, not at kiosks in places open to the public such as bazaars, parks, and railroad stations, but at "closed" kiosks located within enterprises, institutions, and other government buildings. Sales could be made at kiosks on main streets but only in limited numbers. The instruction also noted that there was no need to make efforts to sell all copies because, according to the US-Soviet agreement, the Soviet distributor had the right to return unsold copies to the publisher. For distributors of the magazine throughout the Soviet Union, the message from the party's Central Committee was clear.

---

[26] The recommendations on limiting distribution and entering subscriptions for *Amerika* are in "*O rasprostranenii b CCCP zhurnala 'Amerika'*" (On the Distribution in the USSR of *Amerika* Magazine), 30 July 1956, signed by F. Konstantinov, Head, Department of Propaganda and Agitation, Central Committee of the Communist Party of the Soviet Union. This document can be found at Harvard University's Lamont Library in Fond 89, "Declassified Documents of the Communist Party, 1956," No. 191, *Opis 46, Delo* 11.

Despite such extreme measures, there is ample evidence that *Amerika* had a wide readership in the Soviet Union. On days when the magazine went on sale in Moscow, US embassy officers would check kiosks where they learned that the few token copies found there were usually kept under the counter for preferred customers. On trips around the country, embassy officers found that Soviet citizens they encountered knew about the magazine, and many had seen copies whose covers they were able to describe. Moreover, judging from the dog-eared copies they saw, embassy officers concluded that each copy was read by many readers.

The party instruction that subscriptions be entered at social organizations and institutions was intended to inhibit average Soviet citizens from purchasing the magazine, but it also ensured that the magazine would reach middle- and high-ranking officials who had no such inhibitions. Moreover, the complimentary copies distributed gratis by the American embassy were mailed to officials and other prominent people throughout the Soviet Union. One such official on the embassy mailing list was a young Communist Party secretary in Stavropol named Mikhail S. Gorbachev. To dispose of the "unsold" copies returned to the embassy, they were distributed to embassy contacts and to visitors at the US exhibitions shown in the Soviet Union under the cultural agreement.

The effectiveness of *Amerika* can best be assessed by the extreme measures taken by the Soviet authorities to limits its distribution. There is no doubt that readers were impressed with the standard of living and everyday life in the United States portrayed in the magazine, and they made the inevitable comparisons with their own lives. Produced by a Washington staff of no more than thirty-five at an annual cost of one million dollars (exclusive of salaries), *Amerika* was a minor expense, but a major success, in the cold war of ideas.[27]

Negotiating with the Russians

Negotiating with the Soviets was always an ordeal, especially when cultural exchanges were involved. Of particular concern to

---

[27] The cost estimate of *Amerika* magazine is from John Jacobs, a former chief editor of the magazine, in telecon with author, 11 September 1999.

the Soviets were US exchanges that could influence large numbers of their citizens: our major Public Diplomacy programs such as exhibitions, performing arts, and *Amerika* magazine. Those three were often the most difficult exchanges to reach agreement on, and they often threatened to torpedo the entire cultural agreement.

The US-Soviet cultural agreement initially was renegotiated every two years, and it was usually an ordeal of several weeks duration, longer in Moscow where the Americans could afford to wait out the Soviet negotiators, but shorter in Washington where the Soviets would be spending their dollars for hotel accommodations. Negotiations for the 1968–1969 agreement, for example, were opened in Moscow on 3 June 1968, and the agreement was signed on 15 July after many laborious meetings.[28] Each clause, and often every word, of the agreement was worked over until language was found that was acceptable to both sides.[29] Wording of the agreement was often a problem because some words in English simply did not exist in Russian, or had different meanings.

The US delegation usually was headed by the Director of the Soviet and East European Exchanges Staff in the State Department's Bureau of European Affairs (EUR/SES), and included officers from the State Department, USIA, the American Embassy Moscow, and a representative of the US academic community. The Soviet side was headed by a senior diplomat, usually with the rank of ambassador, from the Cultural Relations Department, USSR Ministry of Foreign Affairs, and included representatives of the various Soviet ministries and agencies that were involved in the exchanges.

USIA's exhibitions were always *the* major source of contention during the negotiations, with the Soviets trying to eliminate them or reduce the number of cities where they were to be shown, while the Americans sought to increase the number of cities or at least maintain the level of the previous agreement. Consequently, exhibitions were usually left to the final

---

[28] For details of the 1967–1969 negotiation, see National Archives and Records Administration, RG 59, Central Files 1967–1969, EDX 4 US-USSR; and Johnson Library, National Security File, USSR, Vols. XX and XXI.

[29] For more on Soviet negotiating tactics, see Chapter 6, "Negotiating with Russians," in Yale Richmond, *From Nyet to Da: Understanding the Russians,* 3rd ed. (Yarmouth, ME and London: Intercultural Press, 2003), 151–66.

days of the negotiation after all other exchanges had been agreed to. In negotiations for the 1972–1973 agreement, the Soviets reluctantly accepted language providing for exhibitions only after US Ambassador Beam personally took the issue to Foreign Minister Gromyko.

Reciprocity *ad absurdum*

Reciprocity was a basic principle in US-Soviet exchanges. But in early 1968, the embassy received a telegram from State informing us that a photo of Soviet Premier Kosygin had been featured on the cover of the 6 February issue of *Life* magazine, and instructing us to request the Soviets to feature Lyndon B. Johnson on the cover of a comparable Soviet magazine. I don't know whether the proposal originated in the White House or USIA, but given the sad state of US-Soviet relations at the time due to the Vietnam war, it was a seemingly impossible task. Nevertheless, I asked for an appointment with the editor of *Ogonek* (*Little Flame*), a leading Soviet weekly, and got it. Accompanied by John Tuohey, our Press Officer at the time, I was received by chief editor Anatoly Sofronov and two others from his staff. Setting the tone for our discussion was a piece of a US fragmentation bomb, a relic of the Vietnam war, placed at the center of the table where we could not fail to see it. With that centerpiece, the meeting degenerated into a discussion of the Vietnam War, and needless to say, we did not accomplish our mission of getting LBJ on the cover of *Ogonek*.

A similarly impossible request came after Svetlana Alliluyeva, Stalin's daughter, had defected to the West and published her memoirs, *Twenty Letters to a Friend*.[30] On that occasion, someone in Washington wanted us to find out what the Soviet "man in the street" was saying about the book. Needless, to say, I did not attempt to interview any Russians about the book.

Invasion of Czechoslovakia

We all remember where we were when important events in history occurred—Pearl Harbor, D-day in Europe, the death of

---

[30] Svetlana Alliluyeva, *Twenty Letters to a Friend* (New York: HarperCollins, 1967).

Franklin D. Roosevelt, the explosion of the atom bomb over Hiroshima, the assassination of John F. Kennedy. But the event I recall most vividly was the Soviet invasion of Czechoslovakia.

It was the end of August 1968, 20 August to be exact, and I was returning to my post in Moscow after a month-long vacation in Finland accompanied by my most precious possessions—my wife and our three small children. And filling out the remaining space in our Plymouth station wagon were the many items we had purchased in Helsinki to make our second year in Moscow more comfortable.

To get an early start on the all-day drive to Moscow, we decided to overnight at a hotel in Hamina, a small town on the Finnish side of the Soviet border, get a good night's sleep, and leave early the next morning for our non-stop return to Moscow.

The next morning, Sunday 21 August, I rose early and went out to check my car and try to find an English-language newspaper. As I stepped out of the hotel lobby onto the town square, I immediately sensed that something was wrong. It was deathly still, with not a person in sight.

Returning quickly to the hotel, I asked the desk clerk what had happened. "The Russians have invaded Czechoslovakia," he somberly said, "and we are all listening to our radios to see if Finland will be next."

The Finns had good reason to be wary of the Soviet Union, having fought two wars with the Russians in the early 1940s. But my concern was not Finland but my wife and three children, and whether we should stay put in neutral Finland or cross the border and return to Moscow.

"What to do?" as the Russians might ask. There I was, with my entire family, on the Finnish side of the Iron Curtain, heading back into the Soviet Union just as a major military confrontation appeared to be developing in the heart of Europe.

My first task was to get the facts, to find out what was really happening. Like the Finns, I turned to radio to assess the situation. Using the short-wave receiver installed in my station wagon, I listened to the Voice of America, BBC, Radio Liberty, the *Deutsche Welle,* and other international broadcasters. They all had plenty of news about movements of the armed forces of the Soviet Union and four of its Warsaw Pact allies, but not much in the way of what the invasion meant for Europe, US-Soviet relations, and whether it signaled the start of World War III.

After listening to the radio reports, my wife and I decided to return to Moscow. Despite the immensity of the invasion, we gambled that it was not going to be the start of another war.

Approaching the border-crossing point at Vaahmaa, it was apparent that the guards on the Soviet side were on high alert. The lines of cars on both sides of the border were much longer than usual, and the Soviet guards were checking passports and vehicles with more than their usual thoroughness.

After a wait of about an hour we were readmitted to the Soviet Union and embarked on our long drive back to Moscow. And so we drove all day and well into the night, going ever deeper into the heart of Russia while listening to increasingly alarming radio reports all the way, and wondering whether we had made the right decision.

The invasion of Czechoslovakia caused a US suspension of high visibility exchanges with the Soviet Union. Scholarly exchanges continued, but there were no exchanges of performing artists or exhibitions. In September, the month following the invasion, the University of Minnesota Concert Band was scheduled to tour the Soviet Union, and the USSR Symphony Orchestra was tuning up for an extensive North American tour, including many performances in the United States. But on instructions from Washington, we had to inform the Soviets that we would not issue US visas for the orchestra.

I was summoned to the Ministry of Culture to meet with Deputy Minister Vladimir I. Popov, who delivered a strong protest. Using a Russian expression, he said the orchestra members were "sitting on their suitcases," waiting for their visas. As for the Minnesota Concert Band whose Soviet tour we had postponed, he asked who would pay for the hotel rooms he had reserved, the posters and programs that had been printed, and the other advance costs that had been incurred by the Ministry. "Charge it up to the costs of invading Czechoslovakia," I replied. It was an honest answer, I thought, but poor Popov became apoplectic, and that was the only time I thought that a Soviet official might hit me. Years later, it fell to me to receive Popov in New York when he headed a Soviet cultural delegation, but all was forgiven and he was full of sweetness and light.

As a consequence of the invasion of Czechoslovakia, the State Department instructed the Moscow Embassy to limit its contacts with the Soviet government. All routine contacts were suspended, and cultural, scientific, and other exchanges conducted under the intergovernmental cultural agreement were put on hold, except for the scholarly exchanges conducted by IREX. If that was intended to "punish" the Soviet Union, I fail to see the logic in such an action that must have pleased Soviet hardliners. The suspension was not lifted until the start of the Nixon administration in early 1969.

August 1968, however, was not a total loss. In that month, the US Congress approved legislation giving USIA officers career status within the Foreign Service. Previously we had been Reserve Officers, subject to dismissal. Now we were full fledged Foreign Service Officers.

Fanfare for Detente

The University of Minnesota Concert Band eventually did tour the Soviet Union, but only in 1969 after the election of President Nixon, and it was a tour that neither the Minnesota musicians nor their Soviet audiences will ever forget.

From Minneapolis to Novosibirsk in Siberia, the furthest stop on their tour, was exactly half way round the world. But most of the band members had never been beyond Minnesota, only one had been as far as the US East Coast, and none had ever been abroad. How would they perform in the big time of the Soviet concert stage? That question troubled me as I met the fifty-four band members at Moscow's Sheremetyevo airport and traveled with them to Leningrad where their seven-week tour of the Soviet Union was to begin.

The Minnesota visit was important because it was the first US cultural exchange in the Soviet Union since the invasion of Czechoslovakia one year earlier, an action that had caused the Johnson administration to suspend all high-visibility Soviet exchanges. In the opening months of the Nixon administration, the tour was intended as a signal that the new administration sought an improvement in US-Soviet relations. In retrospect, the band's tour was the opening fanfare for détente, the process of relaxing tensions between the two superpowers.

Apprehension mounted when the band assembled in Leningrad for a rehearsal on the stage of Philharmonic Hall, home of the Leningrad Symphony, where it was to give its first concert. When the students went on tour in Minnesota they usually performed in high school gymnasiums and National Guard armories. In Leningrad, they were to open in a grand Old World concert hall that dated from 1839 and was renowned for its acoustics. As their first notes bounced back from the rear of the hall, the Minnesotans were awestruck. Some of them told me that they had never heard that kind of sound before, and it was theirs.

The Minnesota troupe was a symphonic band rather than an orchestra, a type of musical ensemble not well known to Soviet audiences. How would the Russians react when their Tchaikovsky, Glinka, and Gliere were played by wind instruments with no strings except a lone double bass?

The Soviet Ministry of Culture was also apprehensive. Under cultural exchange, it was sending its world famous symphony orchestras, ballet companies, and folk dancers to the United States. In return, it had been asked by the State Department to accept student musicians.[31] Was that a legitimate exchange?

Doubts vanished as the Minnesotans, ably led by Maestro Frank Bencriscutto, demonstrated their musical talents in Leningrad, Moscow, and eight other cities during their tour. Soviet critics were impressed by their musicianship, technical mastery, and precision, as well as the high quality of their instruments. Some critics told me that many of the young Minnesotans were good enough to play in Soviet symphony orchestras. And at the end of each concert, when the hall echoed to a medley of Minnesota student songs, the critics learned that the instrumentalists could also sing.

Tuba virtuoso Stanford Freese captured the audience at each performance when he played "Carnival of Venice" and other cornet favorites on his tuba. Back in Minneapolis, Freese played tuba in a jazz combo, and when the conductor of the Novosibirsk Symphony asked him why he did not play in a symphony orchestra, Freese surprised the Russian by replying that he made more money playing jazz.

In Central Asia's legendary Samarkand, which Genghis Khan sacked in 1220 and Tamerlane rebuilt in 1369, the Minnesotans were assured that they could safely leave their instruments overnight on the concert hall stage. The next morning, how-

---

[31] The State Department, with a limited budget for performing arts exchanges, often engaged university musical ensembles because they did not require an honorarium. All of them had successful tours abroad and received favorable reviews.

ever, they discovered that their instrument cases had been opened during the night. It turned out that local musicians could not resist the temptation to try out the band's instruments, the likes of which they had never heard.

Also in Samarkand, a Russian who had too much to drink approached the Minnesotans in a restaurant after their evening performance and belligerently asked why there were no blacks in the band. I invited him to have a drink with me at a neighboring table, and told him that there were not many blacks in Minnesota, which was probably true at the time. Nonplussed by my reply, the drunk next asked how many Jews there were in the band. I happened to know there was one—because he had asked to meet with Soviet Jews—and I told him so. "Aha," he gloated, "in Soviet orchestras we have many Jews," also true at the time. I conceded him points on that one, and we parted friends.

On their return to the United States, the Minnesotans were invited by President Nixon to perform in the White House Rose Garden. In his remarks Nixon expressed his hope that the band's Soviet tour would be followed by more exchanges that would help the Soviet and American people to know each other better so that they could live together, "yes, in rivalry, but in rivalry with the peaceful competition that can only be good for both of us."[32]

Moved by the Movies

American movies were also shown in the Soviet Union, and not just documentary films but feature films, the ones we see in our neighborhood theaters. The cultural agreement provided for the purchase and distribution, on a commercial basis, of films produced in each country, and each year the Soviets purchased, on average, four or five American films that they subtitled or dubbed in Russian and showed in theaters throughout the Soviet Union.[33]

---

[32] Press release, Office of the White House Press Secretary, "Remarks of the President, Dr. Malcolm Moos, Ambassador Anatoly F. Dobrynin, and Ambassador Llewellyn E. Thompson at the concert by the University of Minnesota Band in the Rose Garden, 23 May 1969."

[33] For more details of the film exchange, as well as a history of US film showings in the Soviet Union, see Yale Richmond, *Cultural Exchange and the Cold War*, 128–132, and Hans N. Tuch, *Communicating With the World*, 134–35.

Soviet films were offered to American distributors through Sovexportfilm, the state monopoly for film sales and purchases abroad. With a few exceptions they were not box-office successes in the United States, although their suitability for Western audiences improved over the years as the Soviets learned more about what audiences in the United States and Europe wanted to see.

American films, under the cultural agreement, were offered to the Soviets through the Motion Picture Association of America (MPAA), which represented the major Hollywood studios. Most of those accepted by the Soviets were pure entertainment—comedies, adventure stories, musicals, and science fiction—which met the interests of Soviet audiences. Among the more popular were Some Like It Hot, The Apartment, The Chase, and Tootsie. Also purchased, however, were films of social protest and realistic portrayals of contemporary American life, which Soviet ideologists considered correct in portraying the ills of capitalism. The directors with the largest number of films purchased in those years were Stanley Kramer with seven, and William Wyler with six.

Many of those films, however, were made in the social protest tradition of American literature and were screened by the State Department and given a "no objection" stamp of approval prior to being offered for purchase by the Soviet Union.[34] Such films, nevertheless, helped to satisfy the great curiosity and hunger of Russians for information about the United States. They showed much about American contemporary life and its high standard of living. What may have appeared as poverty to Americans seemed like affluence to Russians. Audiences were not so much listening to the sound track or reading the subtitles as watching the doings of people in the films—in their homes, in stores, on the streets, the clothes they wore, and the cars they drove. And when refrigerators were opened in Western films, they were always full of food. Such details, which showed how people lived in the West, were most revealing for Soviet audiences. When they saw films about Westerners and their problems, their reaction was, "I wish we had their problems."

---

[34] During the early years of the cultural agreement it was common practice for the State Department and USIA to screen MPAA films before they were offered to the Soviet Union. Films produced by independent studios that were not members of MPAA were offered directly to the Soviets.

Although the number of purchased films was small, hundreds of copies were made for distribution in cinemas throughout the Soviet Union. And many of the films that were not purchased by the Soviet Union were clandestinely copied and screened for high-ranking officials and their spouses, and other privileged people of the Soviet Union.

A Hamburger with Khachaturian

An assignment in Moscow provided opportunities to meet prominent and world-famous Soviet citizens, some on business and others in very unusual circumstances. And that's how I came to have a hamburger with Aram Khachaturian, the renowned Armenian composer.

My story begins in 1968 with Ambassador Thompson flying back to Moscow from a visit to Washington and seated next to a woman who began the usual in-flight chit-chat. On learning that Thompson was American ambassador to the Soviet Union, his seat companion began to ply him with questions about his relations with the Russians. Unwilling to discuss political problems with a woman he did not know, Thompson made small talk about life in Moscow.

"What is your most immediate problem?" she eventually asked, and Thompson told her of his unfulfilled plans for the upcoming embassy Fourth of July reception. What he really would like to do, said the Colorado-born and bred diplomat who was definitely not of the striped-pants variety, was to stage a real American cookout for his Soviet guests, with hot dogs, hamburgers, rolls, and all the fixings, which, of course, were unavailable in Moscow at the time.

"Tell me how many guests you plan to have?" replied Joan Toor Cummings, the New York philanthropist and art patron whose husband was the founder and president of Consolidated Foods Corporation (later Sara Lee Corporation), "and I'll have the whole works shipped to you by air."

And so it came about that more than 200 of Moscow's political and cultural elite gathered on July 4 in the garden of Spaso House, the ambassador's residence, where they were introduced to American hamburgers and hot dogs, grilled over charcoal by embassy teenagers. And that's how I found myself standing in line at the charcoal grill with Aram Khachaturian, the celebrated composer, who was waiting patiently for his second hamburger. Khachaturian has been described as "accessibility incarnate," and we chatted.[35] Not about music or high culture, but about hamburgers—which he liked very much—their ingredients, and how they had become the American sandwich par excellence.

Khachaturian, in 1948, had been accused of bourgeois tendencies in his music compositions, but was later rehabilitated and remained in good standing with the Soviet authorities, despite his love of hamburgers. He died before McDonald's opened its first restaurant in Moscow, and *gamburgers,* as they are called in Russian, took Russia by storm. And that's how Mrs. Cummings, the art patron who presented priceless paintings to Chicago's Art Institute and New York's Metropolitan Museum, also brought the plebeian hamburger to Moscow.

Everything Comes to Russia Late

The American hamburger came late to Russia, but so did many other things from the West. With its self-imposed isolation, and its command economy and over-centralization, the Soviet Union was often decades behind developments in other countries. Ideas from the capitalist West were seen as dangerous, and although Russia has produced many great scientists and scholars, the tried and traditional was often preferred over the new and innovative. Moreover, Soviet suspicion of the modern West can be seen as a continuation of an anti-modernism tradition in Russian history. That seemed to be how the Soviet leadership, many of whom were of peasant origin, wanted it.

When Western steel mills were producing lighter and modern steel alloys, the Soviet Union's Lenin Steel Works at Magnitogorsk—seven miles long, and the largest steel plant in the world—was still producing sixteen million tons of steel every year, using the old open-hearth method, and subjecting all the inhabitants of the town to its noxious gases and particulates.

The abacus was still being used in stores to add up purchases when I arrived in Moscow in 1967. Two years later, electronic calculators began to appear in stores, but cautious cashiers, suspicious of innovation, were checking them with an abacus.

---

[35] Bernard Holland, *New York Times,* 14 October 2003.

Twenty-two years later, at a meeting of the Congress of People's Deputies, the Soviet parliament, in May 1989, complaints were made about the shortage of computers, and some Soviet scientists were still using the abacus.

When making purchases in stores, Russians had to stand in line three times. One was to tell a clerk what you wanted and receive a chit with the purchase written on it. The second line was to present the chit to a cashier and make payment. The third line was to present your receipt of payment and pick up your purchase. What Russian, I often wondered, had thought up such a time-consuming and labor-intensive system? But I later observed the same system being used in a Paris department store, and learned that it had been brought to tsarist Russia from France.

In a country that claimed to have given full equality to women, and had enshrined that equality in its constitution, traditional attitudes toward women continued. One day my wife, who was driving our Plymouth station wagon, was stopped by a traffic cop who asked to see her papers. She produced her Soviet driver's license and vehicle registration, but the officer then told her she needed her husband's written permission to drive the car, and he asked to see it.

Gasoline for cars had to be pumped by hand, as it had been in Germany in the late 1940s. So it was a pleasant surprise when the first electric pumps appeared in Moscow. But when I stopped for gas once on the main road from Moscow to Leningrad, the new electric pumps were controlled from the gas station's office, and you had to tell the clerk how many liters you wanted, and pay in advance. If you misjudged the amount of gas your tank could take and it overflowed, there was no way for the customer to stop the pump. Consequently, there were big puddles of gasoline on the ground around the pumps, presenting a severe fire hazard. And when I asked the clerk where I could get some water for my car radiator, she directed me to a well behind the station where I could fetch water in a bucket at the end of a long rope. I did not have to pump my gas, but I did have to haul my water.

Baltic Exchanges

Foreign policy is made in Washington and implemented by our ambassadors abroad, but there are times when embassy officers can change or modify policy. One such opportunity, regarding the US position on the three Baltic states, occurred in 1968.

US policy on Estonia, Latvia, and Lithuania was consistent during the Cold War—their forced incorporation into the Soviet Union was not recognized by the United States, and the three states maintained diplomatic missions in Washington. That policy, however, had its drawbacks; the United States, under a self-imposed restriction, would not send its scholars, performing artists, or exhibitions to the Baltic states under the US-Soviet cultural agreement. But that changed in 1968 when a telegram from the State Department informed our Moscow embassy that an American scholar had applied for an IREX grant to do research in Vilnius, the capital of Lithuania. The scholar was of Lithuanian descent and had the necessary academic and language qualifications to do his research. Would the embassy have any objections to his receiving an IREX grant under the cultural agreement?

Here was one of those infrequent opportunities where a middle-grade field officer had the opportunity to change government policy, and I grasped it. I went to Ambassador Thompson and suggested that, since it was in our interest to have Americans studying in the Baltic states, it was time to change the policy. Thompson agreed, and the ice had been broken, at least for American scholars.

A few years later, when I was serving as Deputy Director of the State Department's Soviet and East European Exchanges Staff, the question arose regarding our policy of not sending US exhibitions and performing artists to the Baltic states. I invited the Joint Baltic American National Committee (JBANC) to discuss the matter, and representatives of the Estonian, Latvian, and Lithuanian communities came to meet with me at the Department. As they sat around my desk, I explained how useful it would be to have American exhibitions and performers in the Baltic states, and asked their opinions. Without any discussion, they all agreed with my proposal but, in deference to hardliners within their own organizations, they cautioned that they did not wish to be quoted as favoring the policy change. And in 1973 the State Department sent the José Limón Dance Company, the first US-sponsored cultural activity in the Baltic states under the cultural agreement.

Press Attaché

When John "Jack" Tuohey, our Press Attaché, completed his tour of duty in summer 1968, and the embassy's Press and Cultural Section was cut one position in a global reduction of US personnel abroad, I assumed his duties.[36] They included maintaining liaison with the twenty-six American correspondents accredited to Moscow, and acting as embassy spokesman.

The American correspondents were a colorful crowd. Among them were such Moscow veterans as Henry Shapiro of UPI, who had arrived in Moscow as a law student in 1933 and worked there as a correspondent, with a few interruptions, from 1934 until his retirement in 1973. Another veteran was Edmund Stevens, a stringer for the London *Sunday Times,* who had won a Pulitzer Prize in 1950 for his coverage of the Soviet Union for the *Christian Science Monitor.* Through the American correspondents it was possible to meet many interesting personalities, Russian and American.

Stevens, and his Russian wife who dealt in underground art, would throw big parties at their palatial home where it was possible to meet prominent people from the cultural scene. At one such evening, I offered a ride home to a couple from the Moscow film studio who lived in one of those apartment buildings reserved for the favored few. When they invited my wife and me up for a drink, we accepted and had a most illuminating insider overview of the Russian film industry.

It was the spokesman's job to respond to inquiries from the press and to ensure that the embassy spoke with one voice on matters of fact and policy. That required handling inquiries from correspondents, determining the embassy position, and passing it to the press. The press attaché was also responsible for the weekly Friday-afternoon background briefings that Ambassador Thompson held for the American press corps. Always well attended, they served to give the American correspondents an insider's view of embassy and Washington thinking on US-Soviet relations.

---

[36] With the shrinking of the US trade surplus, and to reduce the outflow of dollars, the State Department, in 1968, under a program called BALPA (Balance of Payments), requested all US overseas missions to cut a number of personnel positions.

However, there were times when information had to be withheld. Such instances arose, for example, when a US citizen had been detained by Soviet authorities, and the embassy was working to obtain his release and get him out of the Soviet Union without creating an incident that could escalate to a confrontation between the two superpowers. And therein lies an amusing tale.

In those years, the Soviet Union was a transit point for drugs originating in Afghanistan and ending up in Western Europe. One of the vehicles for transiting drugs was a Scandinavian Airways flight that originated in Kabul and made a stop in Moscow en route to Stockholm. Now and then, American citizens bearing drugs were apprehended during their stopover at the Moscow airport. The embassy would work to obtain their release, but the Soviets would then make the matter public by announcing it to the press.

And so, one morning, I received a call from Henry Bradsher, the Associated Press Moscow bureau chief, who asked why I had not told him about a detained American. "Because you did not ask me, Henry," I replied. "Well," said Bradsher, "from now on, whenever I call you on any matter, I will end my call by asking if any Americans are imprisoned in the Soviet Union today."

Bradsher did that for several months whenever he called me, but he eventually got tired of asking, and stopped inquiring. And sure enough, another American was apprehended at the Moscow airport for drug possession, and we went through the same routine once more. Bradsher was not pleased.

More important questions were difficult to evade, and many of them dealt with major issues in US-Soviet relations. On such issues, western correspondents would try to get an embassy statement so they could file a story with a Moscow dateline. To make things more difficult, we knew that President Johnson had three televisions in the Oval Office and, during times of crisis, he would be watching all three—ABC, CBS, and NBC—so that anything the embassy spokesman said might be heard by the president. And if he did not like it, he would let us know.

Jewish emigration and Soviet dissidents were two topics that were an important part of reporting from the Soviet Union in those years, and for foreign correspondents in Moscow they made headlines back home. The dissident movement was slowly building, and there were always a few courageous Russians who were willing to openly defy the communist system and talk with Western correspondents about their defiance. Likewise, Jewish emigration was becoming an issue in US-Soviet relations, and the "refuseniks," as they were called, who were denied permission to emigrate, were intent on making publicity over their misfortune.

Aeroflot

Another hazard in being posted to Moscow was having to fly Aeroflot, the Soviet national airline. The old Aeroflot, which had a monopoly on domestic routes, was not noted for its comfort, convenience, or attention to passengers, nor for its safety.

Delayed departures were common, with no explanation given to passengers waiting in crowded terminals. In-flight food was barely edible, and service almost non-existent. To save fuel, pilots would make banked turns that seemed close to 45 degrees on takeoff. And I recall my first Aeroflot flight, from Kiev to Moscow in 1963, barely above treetop level, it appeared, also to save fuel.

Aeroflot flights were usually fully booked and even overbooked, but foreigners were boarded first, and on overbooked flights ruble-paying Soviet passengers could be bumped for passengers who had paid in foreign currency. And foreign passengers often received special attention.

On a flight from Moscow to Novosibirsk once, my plane had to make an unscheduled landing at Omsk after the Novosibirsk airport was temporarily closed because of bad weather. But Omsk was a closed city, and I was not supposed to be there, even on the airport tarmac. After we had landed at Omsk, a big bus pulled up alongside the plane, and I, the only foreigner on the plane, was invited to board the bus. I saw a diplomatic incident brewing, but instead, at the terminal lounge a glass of freshly brewed tea awaited me while the other passengers had to sit in the crowded plane for more than an hour until the weather over Novosibirsk had cleared.

The tea was good, but safety on Aeroflot was not a priority. Flight attendants did not check to see if passengers were buckled up or seat backs were in an upright position. And I have been on flights with passengers standing in the aisles and smoking during landings, with baggage stacked against emergency exits, and pilots being served vodka in flight. Soviet jokes about Aeroflot were legion. One of them, as translated into English, went: "Quickly and cheaply, Aeroflot will bury you."

I recall a long day spent with an embassy colleague in the Intourist lounge at the Tbilisi (Georgia) airport waiting for a flight to Moscow. We waited all day with nothing to read but pamphlets on Brezhnev and his achievements. An Intourist lady kept exiting the lounge and returning with glasses of vodka and brandy for a rowdy group of men in an adjoining room. Later that night, when the flight had finally been called, we traipsed to the tarmac where a crowd of sullen Soviet passengers surrounded the steps to the plane. "Inostrantsy!" (foreigners), shouted the Intourist lady as we followed her to the plane. Slowly, the crowd parted as we and a few other foreigners passed between them and were the first to board. But that pleasant feeling turned to horror when we recognized the flight crew walking tipsily down the aisle as the same men who had been swilling vodka all day long at the airport.

Fortunately, the new Aeroflot is a completely different airline. No longer a government monopoly, it must now compete with other airlines. New Airbus and Boeing jets have been purchased, and the staff retrained. Food service has improved, customer satisfaction is a priority, and the safety record is exemplary.

Second Jogger in Moscow

Jogging in Moscow, like many things Russian, was an import from the West. The first Moscow jogger, in 1962, was Peter Bridges, a Foreign Service Officer at the American Embassy. And I was the second jogger, in 1967.

At first, I did not pound the pavements. In those years, just behind the embassy on the site now occupied by embassy staff housing there was a small stadium used by a Moscow sports club. And that's where I jogged every day, weather permitting, much to the amusement of the Russians who were practicing their rugby or *futbol* there.

During winter months, when the track was snowed in, I took to the streets and made several circuits around the embassy, with my eyeglasses frosted over in the cold weather, much to the amazement of Russian streetgoers who do not hesitate to tell complete strangers what they think of them. "*C uma soshli?*" (Are you out of your mind?), they would shout at me.

Children or dogs did not run after me, but drunks sometimes did. Once, coming up Bolshoi Devyatinsky Pereulok, the narrow street where the new embassy now stands, a somewhat-inebriated Russian detached himself from a group of serious drinkers congregated around the open-air vodka stand there, and began to jog alongside me. As we rounded the corner onto Tchaikovsky (now Novinsky) Boulevard, we approached the two Russian militsia men standing guard in front of the embassy. They recognized me, but not the surprised jogger at my side whom they promptly apprehended. I wonder what the charge was. Running with the capitalist dogs?

The strangest jogging episode, however, involved the embassy Marine guards. To keep in shape, they would work out in a large room in the basement of the embassy north wing. One morning, with the temperature well below freezing and with snow on the ground, the Marines decided to emerge from their improvised gymnasium and take a few laps out the embassy gateway, along the sidewalk and back in the other gateway, clad only in shorts, tee shirts, and barefoot! The militsia men were aghast, and I always wondered what their KGB chiefs made of that episode and those "crazy Americans."

Foreign Radio Broadcasts

Radio was one of the West's strongest weapons in the Cold War, enabling it to breach the information monopoly held by the Soviet authorities and tell the Soviet people what their own government did not want them to hear. Among the foreign broadcasts beamed to the Soviet Union were those of Radio Liberty (RL) and Voice of America (VOA) from the United States, British Broadcasting Corporation (BBC), the Canadian Broadcasting Corporation (CBC), the *Deutsche Welle* (Germany), *Kol Israel,* and others from France, Italy, and the Vatican.

To counter foreign broadcasts, especially those in Soviet languages, the Russians built a vast network of transmitters that emitted noise, music, or voice on frequencies used by Western broadcasters. Also used were irritating sounds that were psychologically and physically debilitating to listen to over a period of time. The jamming, which made listening difficult, if not impossible, was massive, and its total power was estimated at three times that of all the Western radios combined. Jammers were more effective in large cities, where they were concentrated, but less so in smaller cities and rural areas.

BBC began broadcasting to the Soviet Union in 1946, VOA in 1947, and Radio Liberation (later named Radio Liberty) in 1953. But Soviet jamming began as early as 1948, targeted on different broadcasts at different times, and it continued, with some pauses, until 1988. Radio Liberty was always jammed, but interference with other broadcasters was suspended during times of détente, and reinstated during times of tension. For example, jamming intensified in 1968 after the Soviet invasion of Czechoslovakia, in 1980 after the invasion of Afghanistan, and in 1981 when the Polish communist authorities outlawed the Solidarity movement and proclaimed martial law.

In an attempt to break through this electronic curtain, western broadcasters would often coordinate the timing of their broadcasts to mount a maximum effort, using as many as 100 different frequencies simultaneously for broadcasts to the Soviet Union, and from as many different directions as possible.

To determine whether American broadcasts could be heard despite the jamming, Washington would periodically send a technician to Moscow. Equipped with a radio receiver, the technician would travel in the Soviet Union and monitor the effectiveness of jamming. Results confirmed that in many rural areas foreign broadcasts were often beyond the effective range of Soviet jammers, but in and around major cities it was usually difficult, if not impossible, to understand the broadcasts over the interference. However, the technicians sent by Washington rarely, if ever, spoke Russian, and their evaluation of the radio reception was based on technical observations.

In September 1968, the Moscow embassy was requested by Washington to monitor Radio Liberty broadcasts in the Moscow area for one week. I volunteered to do the job because, as Counselor for Press and Culture, I had an interest in the effectiveness of the broadcasts, but also because I had a degree in electrical engineering, and knew something about radio broadcasts and antennas. Moreover, a few weeks earlier, while on vacation with my family in Finland, I had installed in my station wagon a radio receiver for exactly such a task.

For seven consecutive nights, I drove around various districts of Moscow listening to Radio Liberty broadcasts, wrote down the news headlines I heard in Russian, where I had heard them, the time of the broadcasts, and their radio frequencies. I was not tailed on those evenings and my work was not hindered in any way although once my monitoring was interrupted by a Soviet militsia man who asked what I was doing parked on a side street on the outskirts of Moscow. "Listening to American radio broadcasts," I replied, "because jamming prevents me from listening to them in our embassy in midtown Moscow." That honest answer seemed to satisfy him, much to my relief.

Returning to the embassy, I sent the results of each evening's work by telegram to the State Department and Radio Liberty in Munich, proving that Liberty's broadcasts could indeed be heard in most parts of Moscow and understood above the jamming, if one had a decent receiver, knew something about antennas, and understood Russian.

When I returned to the United States at the end of my tour, I was invited to call on Howland H. Sargeant, President of the Radio Liberty Committee in New York, who thanked me for my efforts.[37] Sargeant told me that Radio Liberty broadcasts had been threatened with closure by Congress unless it could be shown that they could be heard above the jamming, and my monitoring had saved the day. Sargeant wrote a letter (on 11 December 1969) to Henry Loomis, USIA Deputy Director, to that effect, which was placed in my personnel file.

Music and Theater Critic

Moscow had much more to offer in addition to interesting work. For Americans who could speak some Russian, the cultural scene was rich—in music, dance, and theater—and tickets were cheap and readily available for diplomats.

Blocks of tickets were reserved for visiting dignitaries each day by the Ministry of Foreign Affairs. By 5 p.m., unneeded tickets for that evening would be offered to the diplomatic corps, and a Soviet employee in our administrative section would tell us what was available. A quick telephone call to my wife would determine what we wanted to see that evening, and by 5:30 p.m. we would be in our car on the way to a performance. Park-

---

[37] This is the same Howland H. Sargeant who was married to Hollywood film star Myrna Loy.

ing was never a problem in those years, even in downtown Moscow, and in fifteen minutes I could pull up to the Bolshoi or another theater, park my car at the curb, and enter the building. After a *buterbrod* (sandwich) at the theater *bufet* (snack bar), we would be in our seats for a 6 p.m. performance.

During my last year in Moscow, I learned to play theater and music critic. Whenever I attended a performance that was culturally or politically interesting, I would return to the embassy after the performance, draft a report, and send it by priority telegram to the State Department, USIA, and Radio Liberty in Munich, Germany, for broadcast back to the Soviet Union the next day. I don't know if the KGB ever learned the identity of that phantom arts critic.

Was it possible to have Russian friends? It was indeed possible, but you had to understand that any Russian who associated with Americans would be interrogated by the KGB and could be subject to pressure to participate in a *provokatsia* (provocation). Indeed, some Americans who thought they had made friends with Russians found that their "friends" had helped to entrap them in provocative situations that caused their prompt departure from the Soviet Union for their own protection. And yet there were some Russians who defied the authorities, like the dissident writer Andrei Amalrik who had the courage to come to my apartment in the embassy, and to invite me to visit him in the small room he shared in a communal apartment with his lovely wife, Guzel, an expressionist painter. Amalrik, in the title of his book, *Will the Soviet Union Survive Until 1984?* missed his mark by only a few years.[38] Unfortunately, he himself did not survive beyond 1980, when he was killed in an automobile accident in Spain on his way to a human rights meeting in Madrid.

Travels in the Soviet Union

Moscow was the capital of the Soviet Union, the largest country in the world, two and one-half times larger than the United States, extending 6,000 miles from West to East, and encompassing eleven time zones. But while Moscow was the center

---

[38] Andrei Amalryk, *Will the Soviet Union Survive Until 1984?* (New York: Harper and Row, 1970).

of Soviet power and where the action was, the rest of the country, in many ways, was more interesting, and where one could see the real Russia—influenced more by the past than the present. Whenever an opportunity for travel to the provinces arose, embassy officers took it.

Georgia was everyone's favorite, for Russians as well as Americans. The Caucasus Mountain scenery is striking, the weather mild, and the wine and food delicious. But it is the legendary Georgian hospitality that is remembered most.

Cooking is an art in Georgia, and so is dining. Food is eaten leisurely, and dinners can last several hours as the various courses keep coming. Moreover, previous courses are not removed, so that in short time the table is laden with big platters of food that had been offered earlier and are piled up high on top of the others.

At each dinner, a *tamadan* (toastmaster) is designated who presides over the dinner and offers a toast with each serving of food or drink. And the toast is not a mere "Cheers" or "To your health," but rather a speech praising the quality of the food or wine, the generosity of the host, the beauty and charm of his wife, the future of their children, or a prophetic comment on the occasion for the gathering. Toasting is an art form in Georgia, and a guest will be judged by the quality of his toasts. After a few of those Georgian dinners, I learned to always have a few lengthy toasts ready to deliver.

Georgia is also a man's world, or at least it was when I visited there years ago. At those festive dinners women were not seated at the table, but were relegated to the kitchen where they cooked, and from where they emerged only to serve the male guests. At one such serving, when I was offered a dish I had never seen before, I inquired of my table partner, "What is it?" To which the woman bearing the food tray replied in perfect English, "Try it, you'll like it."

"Who was that?" I inquired of the man seated to my left after she had passed on to the next guest. "Oh, she is professor of English at our university," he replied.

On one of my many visits to Leningrad (now St. Petersburg), I planned to call on the *rektor* (president) of Leningrad State University, and bring him a gift, a 30-minute film of one of NASA's Apollo moon missions. Embassy Moscow had received the film from USIA, but had no way of showing it to Soviet science audiences, nor was it likely that Moscow TV would air a film on American achievements in space. However, the rektor of Leningrad State University, Kirill Kondratyev, was a renowned astrophysicist who would certainly appreciate the film. Accordingly, in Leningrad I made an unannounced call on the rektor and was received by him without any hassle. After a few introductory remarks, I presented the Apollo film as a gift of the American Embassy. A few weeks later I heard that Kondratyev had been showing the film to scientists in Leningrad, and the demand to see the film was so great that there were disturbances at some showings with uninvited guests trying to get in. It was another small but important Public Diplomacy achievement.

Novosibirsk is the largest city in Siberia, and interesting to visit because the further one got from Moscow, the less the control from the center and the more outspoken the people were. But Novosibirsk was also home to the Siberian Academy of Sciences, and that is how I came to visit the director of the library of the Siberian Academy. I simply walked in, introduced myself to a person at the entrance, and asked to see the director. Surprised but obviously pleased by my visit, he received me graciously in his office. Traditional Russian hospitality showed itself when he asked his secretary to bring us something to eat and drink. She returned in a few minutes with a loaf of good black bread, some spicy sausage, an old kitchen knife, a bottle of vodka, and two glasses, and our conversation warmed with our stomachs as we sat at his desk eating and drinking—without plates, forks, or napkins—discussing libraries and book exchanges between our countries. His main complaint was that most of the scientific books that the Soviet Union received from abroad remained in Moscow and were never seen in Siberia.

The KGB

No account of the Soviet Union would be complete without mention of the KGB, the Russian acronym for the Committee for State Security—which Americans might call the secret police—the domestic branch of which enforced the decisions of the Communist Party and the Soviet government.

For Americans in Moscow, the KGB was everywhere. It monitored our phone calls in the office and at home, followed some of us around the city and in our travels, staffed many of the Soviet offices where we did official business, and from time to time attempted to entrap us in illegal activities or compromising personal positions.

My wife, for example, was interested in modern art, and made the rounds of artist studios. On two occasions, she was set up for a rendezvous at the apartment of an art dealer, ostensibly to see some interesting paintings, but more likely to become the victim of an entrapment. On both occasions she had the good sense to take me along, which surely disappointed the KGB plotters.

Were our phone conversations recorded? Embassy personnel who lived in an apartment building outside the embassy compound reported that every morning a Russian would climb the stairs for a brief visit to the attic, presumably to collect the tapes from the previous day's monitoring. If that sounds far-fetched, there is also the story of American staffers aboard a Russian plane during one of the Nixon-Brezhnev summit meetings. A sign on the lavatory door read "temporarily closed," but when an American had to go and entered the lavatory, he found a Russian technician seated there, not with his pants down but with his earphones on. And an embassy wife once picked up her apartment phone to make a call but instead heard a recording of a call she had made the previous day.

And old habits die hard. Construction of a new American embassy building was halted in 1986 when American technicians found that, although preventive measures had been taken, the building was riddled with Soviet listening devices. As a result, completion of the building was delayed several years while Congress and the State Department debated whether to try to remove all the listening devices or simply tear down the building and start all over again. Construction was resumed in 1996, and the new embassy building was finally occupied in May 2000.[39] Thirty-one years earlier, I had been asked by the State Department to tell them by priority telegram how many rooms the cultural section would need in the new embassy.

On a flight from Tbilisi to Moscow once, on which seats were preassigned, I found myself seated next to a Russian who was

---

[39] A complete account of the bugging of the embassy construction can be found in Jack F. Matlock, Jr., *Reagan and Gorbachev: How the Cold War Ended* (New York: Random House, 2004), 254–56.

unusually friendly and engaged me in conversation in English, French, and German, three languages in which he and I were conversant. We talked about many things but I kept my guard up, aware that he was probably on a provocative mission. Sure enough, within a few days, he called me at the embassy and asked to be invited to one of the embassy's film showings so he could keep his English up to date. Any Russian who had the audacity to call the embassy with such a request had to be calling for the KGB.

Did I know any KGB agents? Actually, I knew quite a few, and one of them was my neighbor in Moscow. Most of the Soviet officials I worked with on exchanges were believed to be KGB operatives. When I asked one of them, a man I saw regularly at the Ministry of Foreign Affairs, if I could have his home phone number so I could call him on weekends should there be an emergency, he replied that he was at his dacha on weekends and not available. A few months later, the official's wife was assigned to accompany a female Soviet musician on a solo tour of the United States, and when I saw her visa application, I learned that she and her husband were living in a building right next door to the American embassy where I lived. In an emergency, I could have walked over and knocked on the door to his apartment.

Many Soviet officials I dealt with, however, were intelligent as well as intelligence officers. They were easier to talk with, and more open and confident in what they could say to an American diplomat. And some could be helpful at times.

Valentin M. Kamenev, the Soviet cultural counselor in Washington during the 1970s, reportedly a GRU (military intelligence) officer, gave me many tips on how to maneuver my way through the Soviet bureaucracy. Another Soviet official gave me useful information on Soviet tactics during one of the periodic negotiations of the cultural agreement. At a Moscow reception, a KGB official advised me that there was a conversation going on at the other end of the room which I would find interesting, as it indeed was. And at an official lunch in Moscow during the closing years of the Brezhnev regime, a KGB officer had the audacity to tell me that what was wrong with the Soviet Union was that it was governed by a bunch of old men.

Was I followed by the KGB? Not that I was aware of, and in Moscow I learned to be aware of such things. I had previously served in four foreign posts, and the Soviets certainly knew by that time that I was a cultural officer and nothing more. Everything I did was in the open, and I made sure that the Soviets knew whom I was seeing, and when.

Were Americans bothered by Soviet surveillance and wiretaps? Our military attachés, who were usually tailed, certainly were, as were CIA officers serving under diplomatic cover. But that was part of the espionage game, and the Americans understood that their Soviet counterparts in the United States were subject to similar surveillance by the FBI. As for myself, I never let it bother me.

Moscow was a good assignment and I thought it would be the pinnacle of my Cold War odyssey, but the best was yet to come—an assignment at the State Department during the Nixon-Kissinger détente years. But first came a diversion that almost ended my Foreign Service career—a head-on collision with Frank Shakespeare, the new director of USIA.

Chapter 9

SHAFTED BY SHAKESPEARE

Frank Shakespeare, the newly appointed director of the USIA, came to the Soviet Union in June 1969 to open a USIA exhibition, "Education USA," in Leningrad. Shakespeare, a former CBS television executive, had advised Richard Nixon during his presidential campaign and was rewarded with the USIA post.[1] A staunch anti-Communist, Shakespeare had been a member of the college conservative group, Young Americans for Freedom (YAF), and was a friend of columnist William F. Buckley, Jr. In coming to Leningrad, Shakespeare was the first high-ranking official of the new administration to visit the Soviet Union since the inauguration of President Nixon in January of that year. As customary with such VIP visits, he was given a preview of the education exhibition before it formally opened. That preview was to be the first of three strikes against me.

What caught Shakespeare's attention in the exhibition was a collection of books on American education. One by one he went through them and pulled out those he thought should not be shown in the Soviet Union. I asked Wallace W. Littell, USIA's Assistant Director for the Soviet Union and Eastern Europe, who was traveling with Shakespeare, whether we should question Shakespeare on why he wanted those books removed. Littell replied that we have to go through such book bannings with many new USIA directors, so we might as well do it now.[2]

---

[1] See Joe McGinniss, *The Selling of the President 1968* (New York: Trident Press, 1969).

[2] Less than a year later, as reported in *The Washington Post* (25 April 1970), Shakespeare sent a ten-page list of books by conservative authors to each of

Accordingly, at the end of the exhibition walkthrough, we convened in a room that the American exhibition guides used as a lounge. Our little group included Shakespeare; Edward "Teddy" Weintal, his éminence grise; Littell; Jaroslav "Jerry" Verner, our Moscow embassy cultural officer; Thomas L. Craig, the American director of the exhibition; and myself. And there we asked Shakespeare why he objected to books that had been selected by his staff in Washington.

Shakespeare went through the books in question and focused on two collections of photos that were to be used as teachers' aides in explaining to elementary school students the differences between life in the city and the countryside. One of the photos in the city book showed the back alley of a New York City tenement, apparently in the 1920s or earlier, which featured a smiling little boy sitting fully clothed in an abandoned white porcelain bathtub. Shakespeare claimed that the photo showed the United States in an unfavorable light, and that was not USIA's mission.[3]

Verner pointed out that Soviet viewers of the photo, many of whom did not have bathtubs in their apartments, would see it differently. To them, the photo would show that the United States was so wealthy that porcelain bathtubs were abandoned in back alleys. And so it went, from photo to photo, and book to book, with Shakespeare becoming more and more outspoken in his criticism, and the rest of us explaining how the photos and books would look to Soviets. Finally, Shakespeare pointed a finger directly at me, and said, in a room that we assumed had to be bugged by the KGB, that our mission was to overthrow the Soviet government, and anyone who did not understand that did not belong in USIA.

That was a very damaging statement by the first cabinet-level member of the new Nixon administration to visit the Soviet Union, and with full disregard for my career I replied in a firm and loud voice, so it was sure to be picked up by a bugging

---

USIA's 200 overseas libraries with instructions that librarians should order from the list, within forty-eight hours of receipt, if their existing collections were preponderantly liberal. Among the recommended authors were Ronald Reagan, William F. Buckley, Jr., Barry Goldwater, Ayn Rand, and Whittaker Chambers.

[3] Shakespeare's position was the exact opposite of Edward R. Murrow's, USIA's most distinguished director, who thought that the agency should tell America's story to the world, "warts and all."

device, "Mr. Shakespeare, that has never been the policy of the State Department and never will be. Our aim is to live with these people in peace." Shakespeare first flushed, and then blanched before being hustled out of the building and calmed down by Littell.[4]

The Soviet leadership at that time was very apprehensive about the policies that the new Nixon administration might pursue, and anything that Shakespeare would say in that regard was obviously of great interest to the Moscow leadership. What I did in the US national interest and without regard for my career, I later learned, was held against me.

My second confrontation with Shakespeare—and strike two—came a few days later in Moscow at a performance by the Tamburitzans, a folk song and dance ensemble from Pittsburgh's Duquesne University that was touring the Soviet Union under the US-USSR cultural agreement. The highly acclaimed "Tammies," as they are called, usually performed East European folk dances, but at the request of the State Department they had put together a retrospective show of American song and dance, from early colonial days to modern times, culminating in a final number titled "Discotheque," which featured rock music and dance. It was to be the second tour of the Soviet Union by an American performing arts ensemble after the new Nixon administration had lifted the US embargo on cultural exchanges following the Soviet invasion of Czechoslovakia the previous summer. The State Department and the American Embassy wanted the tour to go well.

When we had first proposed to send the Tammies to the Soviet Union, the Soviets were bothered by the title of the final number, "Discotheque," and it had taken considerable tenacity by me and my staff to bring them around to signing a contract with the embassy. To do so, I had agreed, with State Department concurrence, that the Soviets would have an opportunity to review a dress rehearsal prior to opening night. That preview performance took place in Leningrad where the tour was to start, and where they gave a dress rehearsal for local officials. After the performance, the officials, a group of middle-aged men all wearing dark suits, went into a huddle at the rear

---

[4] For further details of this encounter, see Yale Richmond, *Foreign Affairs Oral History Collection* (Washington, D.C.: Georgetown University Library, 9 June 2003), 78. Also online at http://memory.loc.gov/ammem/collections/diplomacy.

of the hall, deliberated for a while, and pronounced the show fit for performance.

Moscow was the next stop on the tour, and on opening night there the first rows of the theater were filled with high-ranking officials of the Soviet Ministry of Culture, including Mme Yekaterina Furtseva, the Minister. But the following morning, I was called to Goskontsert for a meeting with Deputy Director Golovin, who read me the riot act and protested that the Moscow performance was not the one that had been approved in Leningrad. He specifically demanded that one male dancer stop moving his hips so suggestively. Apparently, what was approved in Leningrad, the most Western of Russian cities, did not pass muster in Moscow, the seat of government and the Communist Party.

Accordingly, I informed Tammy Director Walter W. Kolar that he should instruct his dancers to tone down the hip movements in Moscow. I added, however, that once the troupe left Moscow for other cities, no one would care about the hip movements. I did not anticipate any problems, but how wrong I was.

Shakespeare attended the second Moscow performance and, when it had ended, I escorted him backstage to congratulate the dancers. After he had addressed the group, Kolar told Shakespeare that the performance had been even better before it had been "censored." Shakespeare, very concerned, asked who had instructed them to make changes, and Kolar pointed an accusing finger at me. I was unable to persuade either Shakespeare or Kolar that the Soviet request to tone down the hip movements had more to do with Russian prudery than with communist ideology. And I found it strange that a Catholic college dance group had to be told that its performance was considered too sexy.[5]

My third confrontation with Shakespeare—and strike three— occurred a few weeks later in Vienna, where he had convened a meeting of USIA officers from Eastern Europe and the Soviet Union. It was ten months after the Soviet invasion of Czechoslovakia, and our ambassador in Vienna, Douglas MacArthur II, in addressing us, related that political refugees from Czecho-

---

[5] I later learned that the State Department had similar problems with other US performing arts groups in subsequent years, and had to persuade them to tone down their hip movements in Moscow.

slovakia had told him that if there were free elections there, the Socialists or Social Democrats would win.

Shakespeare interjected that we had experts on Eastern Europe in the room, and he asked us what would result from free elections in each of our countries. As he put it, referring to the popular former communist leader of Czechoslovakia, would the people choose Dubcek-style communism or American free-enterprise capitalism?[6]

One by one, my colleagues from their posts in Bulgaria, Czechoslovakia, Hungary, Poland, Romania, and Yugoslavia said that in their countries a free election would be won by Dubcek-style communism or some kind of socialism or social democracy. Shakespeare was shocked, reported *Time* magazine, and asked, "You mean you don't think they'd choose a US-style democracy?"[7]

And then everyone turned to me, the last to answer Shakespeare's question. I began by noting that the Soviet Union was much different from Eastern Europe. In the Soviet Union, I pointed out, there was no democratic tradition. The Communist Party had been in power for more than fifty years and had effectively eliminated all opposition. The average Soviet citizen, I added, associated the Communist Party with Soviet achievements and patriotism, and especially the victory over Nazi Germany in World War II. While most Soviet citizens would like to see a more effective and less harsh communist government, I predicted that in a free election, if such were possible in the Soviet Union, the communists would win.

Columnist and writer William F. Buckley, Jr., a member of the USIA Advisory Committee who was at the meeting as a guest of Shakespeare, immediately challenged my statement because it was incomprehensible to him, and to Shakespeare, that anyone would freely vote communist.

In subsequent years I put the same question to leading US specialists on the Soviet Union, who all said they would have given the same response. And although it saddens me to see people vote communist, recent public opinion polls show that one-quarter or more of Russian adults say they would definitely or probably vote for Stalin were he alive today and running for president, and less than 40 percent say they definitely

---

[6] *Time*, 5 December 1969, 40.

[7] Ibid.

would not. Moreover, as those polls show, reverence for Stalin is found today among the young as well as the old.[8]

After those three encounters with Mr. Shakespeare, it was obvious that with three strikes against me, I was "out" and would not be returning to Moscow for a third year as planned. Moreover, Shakespeare inserted in my personnel file a memorandum (dated 4 January 1970) stating that, in his view, my overall performance was negative, and I did not have "a basic understanding of the substantive issues between communism and the free world."

Also removed from their posts were several other East European public affairs officers, as well as Wallace W. Littell, USIA Assistant Director for the Soviet Union and Eastern Europe, because he refused to acquiesce in Shakespeare's decision to remove me and the others from our posts. Littell was assigned to Belgrade and replaced by his deputy who carried out Shakespeare's request.[9]

In a telegram from Embassy Moscow to USIA Director Shakespeare, Ambassador Beam requested Shakespeare to pass the following message from him to Yale Richmond:

> It was with great reluctance that I released you to the Senior Officer's Course [Senior Seminar], which is an enviable assignment. I want to thank you for the invaluable assistance you have given me in two difficult posts, which will be reflected in your record. We shall miss you very much and send our best to you and the family.[10]

Beam also submitted an Officer Evaluation Report in which he described me as a "first-class Cultural and Public Affairs Officer" with "excellent judgment" and "direct, incisive, and courageous in presenting his views."[11]

---

[8] Sarah E. Mendelson and Theodore P. Berger, "Failing the Stalin Test," *Foreign Affairs*, (January/February 2006).

[9] See Wallace W. Littell, *Foreign Affairs Oral History Collection* (Washington, D.C.: Georgetown University Library, 1 October 1992), 45, or Frontline Diplomacy, Manuscript Division, Library of Congress, Washington, D.C. Also online at http://memory.loc.gov/ammem/collections/diplomacy.

[10] Embassy Moscow telegram 4102, 7 August 1969, to USIAC for Director Shakespeare.

[11] Officer Evaluation Report for Yale W. Richmond, 20 August 1969, signed by Jacob D. Beam, Ambassador.

With the Shakespeare memorandum in my file, and despite uniformly superior Officer Evaluation Reports by all my supervisors, I was passed over for promotion for five years, and was not promoted to Class 1 (FSO-1) until 1974, a year after Shakespeare had resigned as Director of USIA.

For several years there were reports that Shakespeare had interfered in the promotion process for USIA's Foreign Service Officers. Those reports were confirmed in 1971 when the American Foreign Service Association (AFSA), which also represented most of USIA's Foreign Service personnel, protested Shakespeare's right to have final authority over key promotions, claiming that it would introduce partisan politics into the promotion process and destroy the twenty-two-year-old merit system. Under that system, Foreign Service personnel, as in the military services, are graded each year by peer panels and recommended in rank order for promotion. But in an order dated 11 November 1971, Shakespeare said that he wanted promotion boards to submit their recommendations, not in the order recommended for promotion, but in alphabetical order so that he would be free to select candidates he considered best qualified for promotion.[12] Or to pass over those, such as myself, whom he did not want to see promoted.

Shakespeare's hardline politics regarding the Soviet Union eventually led to disagreements with the State Department and the White House. During the Middle East crisis of 1970, when efforts to start Arab-Israeli negotiations were in a delicate stage and the State Department was seeking to avoid antagonizing the Soviets, USIA sent a policy guidance to its overseas posts that took a tough anti-Soviet stand. As a result, Secretary of State William P. Rogers sent Shakespeare a memorandum reminding him that in policy matters USIA was under the authority of the State Department.[13]

Over the following year, things went from bad to worse. Shakespeare scheduled a meeting in Tokyo of USIA Far East officers to discuss ways to contain Communist China, but the meeting had to be canceled when President Nixon announced his plans to visit China.[14] The final blow came when Congress

---

[12] For a full account of this contretemps, see the *Washington Post,* 27 November 1971.

[13] *Washington Post,* 19 October 1970.

[14] *Washingtn Post,* 2 January 1972.

slashed USIA's budget request. As the *Washington Post* editorialized, there was talk on Capitol Hill that the budget cut was Senator Fulbright's revenge for a statement made on television by Bruce Herschenson, USIA's motion picture director and a political appointee, in which he called Mr. Fulbright "naive and stupid." As the *Post* put it, "In the near background, of course, was Mr. Shakespeare's well publicized intent—offensive and properly so, to Mr. Fulbright—to make USIA an arm of militant anti-Communism, in a period otherwise ostensibly dedicated to detente."[15] Shakespeare subsequently, in a letter to Fulbright, apologized for the insulting remarks.[16]

With USIA's status declining, and détente with the Soviet Union and China looming, Shakespeare resigned in December 1972. And Richard Nixon, as president, went on, together with Henry Kissinger, not to overthrow the Soviet government, but to embark on a policy of détente based on cooperation rather than confrontation. That détente was to be the focus of the remaining years of my Foreign Service career.

[15] *Washington Post,* 24 April 1972.
[16] *Washington Post,* 31 March 1972.

Chapter 10

DOING DÉTENTE AT THE DEPARTMENT

The State Department was an exciting place to work in the 1970s, the years of détente with the Soviet Union. But to get to State, I had to take a few detours in my career assignments. The first detour was a nine-month sabbatical (1969–1970) at the Senior Seminar in Foreign Policy—a State Department think tank, similar to the National War College, but conducted by State's Foreign Service Institute. The seminar brought together each year twenty-five senior officers from State, USIA, USAID, CIA, Commerce, and other government agencies, and one each from the four military services.[1] The year I attended, the emphasis was on acquainting members with the changes in the United States that had occurred during their years of service abroad. To do that, we brought in a prominent speaker every morning for a lecture on an American issue of the day followed by a discussion. And for one week each month we traveled to various parts of the United States. It was a prestigious assignment, a great experience, and my consolation prize for having been shafted by Shakespeare.

Another plus for the Senior Seminar was the opportunity to do a research project on some topic on the United States or a foreign country that we had never visited. I chose India and the future of the English-language press in that multilingual country, a project that enabled me to travel around India for three weeks and interview editors and writers in several major

---

[1] In 2004, after forty-six sessions, the Senior Seminar was terminated for budgetary reasons and replaced by shorter courses for a larger number of officers.

cities. My conclusion, not surprisingly, was that, considering the many languages spoken by India's many ethnic groups, the English-language press was a necessity and had a promising future.

After the Senior Seminar, I spent a year (1970–1971) as Policy Officer in the European office of USIA—a strange assignment for someone who, according to Shakespeare, did not have "a basic understanding of the substantive issues between communism and the free world." But then, in 1971, Richard T. Davies, a Deputy Assistant Secretary of State for European Affairs, asked me to come back to State to be Deputy Director of the Soviet and East European Exchanges Staff, EUR/SES, as it was known in State Department shorthand.

EUR/SES, as discussed in an earlier chapter, was the focal point for all US government exchanges with the Soviet Union and Eastern Europe. It did not have a budget for exchanges, but it provided political clearance for exchanges conducted by US government agencies, as well as advice to the private sector when so requested. With the Soviet Union, it also negotiated the renewal of the cultural agreement every two years (later three). Its bread-and-butter work, however, was the approval of visas for all exchange visitors from the Soviet Union and Eastern Europe. I had earlier served three years (1963–1966) there as Officer-in-Charge of East European exchanges, and knew the work well. With détente looming, it promised to be an exciting and important assignment.

With détente and a series of Nixon-Brezhnev summit meetings in the early 1970s, the number of Soviet and East European visitors to the United States increased dramatically. Prior to détente, such visitors from the Soviet Union each year seldom totaled more than 1,000, depending on the number of symphony orchestras or athletic teams that came in any one year. But that number more than doubled with the signature, during the early 1970s, of eleven US-Soviet agreements for cooperation in various fields of science and technology.[2] For each agreement, a joint commission was established, cochaired by

---

[2] At the Nixon-Brezhnev summit meetings during the early 1970s, the United States and the Soviet Union signed eleven agreements for cooperation in Environmental Protection, Science and Technology, Medical Science and Public Health, Space, Agriculture, World Ocean Studies, Transportation, Atomic Energy, Artificial Heart Research and Development, Energy, and Housing and Other Construction.

cabinet-level officials of the two countries, which met annually to review the cooperative activities of the past year and make plans for the future. Altogether, some 240 working groups of US and Soviet scientists were formed to carry out the actual scientific work, which meant that each year some 1,000 Soviet scientists and technicians would visit the United States, and 1,000 Americans would go to the Soviet Union. The visits were only for one or two weeks, but not all the time was spent in the labs. The Soviets were entertained in the homes of their American counterparts, and saw how they lived and played. It was Public Diplomacy at its most intimate.

Détente also encouraged exchanges between US non-governmental organizations (NGOs) and organizations in Eastern Europe, especially with Poland, Hungary, and Czechoslovakia— three countries with big science communities. Exchanges with Eastern Europe and the Soviet Union became very popular, and with encouragement from the White House, almost every government agency, as well as many non-governmental entities, wanted a piece of the action. A good part of each day at EUR/SES was spent explaining to governmental and private organizations exactly how to go about starting an exchange with the Soviet Union.

Often, our expertise and experience was called upon by many in the US government who were following the White House lead in initiating exchanges with the Soviet Union. Even the National Security Council (NSC), under Henry Kissinger, had to call on us once for advice. The NSC had been using its "back channel" through the Soviet embassy to negotiate an agreement for cooperation in science and technology. But when NSC came up against problems they could not resolve, they had to come to EUR/SES for advice, after first swearing us to secrecy on their plans for the new agreement.

I also had the opportunity to participate in the negotiation of two of the cooperative agreements that were an important element in the Nixon-Kissinger détente policy. As a member of a delegation that traveled to Moscow in 1972, I helped to negotiate the agreement on cooperation in environmental protection, the first of the eleven cooperative agreements. My instructions from Deputy Assistant Secretary Davies were to ensure that the agreement contained a clause referring to the US-Soviet cultural agreement, which would give the State Department some say in the environmental agreement and, more important, establish a precedent for other cooperative agreements with the Soviets to be signed by US government agencies.

The Moscow negotiations on environmental protection were held with the USSR State Committee on Science and Technology (GKNT). Environmental protection was a non-controversial issue in US-Soviet relations, and agreement was easily reached on all the environmental questions, but the Soviet negotiators balked at including a reference to the US-USSR cultural agreement. I was the only member of the US team pushing that issue, and when it was clear that we had reached an impasse, the head of the Soviet negotiators announced that we would have to refer the question to their higher-ups. Accordingly, the entire US delegation was received by Dzherman Gvishiani, the GKNT Deputy Director, a suave and sophisticated Georgian with a perfect command of English. Gvishiani was also a son-in-law of Soviet Premier Kosygin, which further enhanced his authority.

Gvishiani received us with his usual charm, and after initial pleasantries he asked if the reference to the cultural agreement was a firm requirement of the US negotiators. Although I was not the head of the US delegation, I immediately replied that it was, and Gvishiani, to our great surprise, simply said, "Then we will have to accept it." And thus it came about that the environmental agreement signed at the Nixon-Brezhnev 1972 summit meeting, as well as the other ten cooperative agreements, all included a reference to the cultural agreement. Mission accomplished.

My other mission to Moscow came in July 1972 with the negotiation of the program for the agreement on cooperation in science and technology (S&T). The agreement, containing general terms, had been signed at the Nixon-Brezhnev summit in May, but still to be negotiated were the much more important actual projects for cooperation. I was one of two State Department representatives on a team of scientists headed by Dr. Edward E. David, Jr., science adviser to President Nixon. David's negotiating partner was GKNT chairman V.A. Kirillin, who was also a Deputy Chairman of the USSR Council of Ministers, i.e., a deputy prime minister.

Plenary sessions were chaired by David and Kirillin but the details of the negotiations were carried out by a working group that included Norman Neureiter of the NSC staff; Eugene E. Fubini, a brilliant scientist who was a consultant to the Department of Defense; John V. Granger, an electrical engineer from

State's Bureau of International Science and Technology; Jack Teck, our Moscow Embassy science attaché; and myself. At one point in our negotiations there occurred one of those rare events that serve to introduce some levity to negotiating in Moscow.

We were negotiating in the GKNT building on Gorky Street (now Tverskaya Street), a center of Soviet intelligence from where Soviet Colonel Oleg V. Penkovsky had passed military secrets to Western intelligence for many years before he was caught and executed. From an upper floor of that building, our embassy attaché Jack Teck wanted to pass a message to his embassy driver waiting far below on a side street adjacent to the building. But for Teck to exit the building and then reenter through the security controls would have been too time-consuming. So, to the astonishment of the Soviet negotiators, who looked on with great interest, Teck wrote his message on a sheet of paper, fashioned it into a glider—the kind we used to throw in school classrooms when the teacher's back was turned—caught the attention of his driver, and dispatched the missile to him from a top floor window of the building. What onlookers down below must have thought as the message gracefully glided down into the outstretched hands of the embassy driver is difficult to determine.

Less challenging at State, but equally important, were the many calls we received from NGOs inquiring how they could initiate exchanges with the Soviet Union. I spent a good part of every day responding to such phone calls and giving advice to Americans how they could do so. Most of the inquirers had interesting exchange proposals in mind, but some appeared frivolous. One call from a state Bar Association, for example, asked how they could invite a Russian lawyer to their annual meeting. "Do you have a particular lawyer in mind?" I inquired. "No," was the response, "we'll take anyone."

International Visitors

After two years at EUR/SES, I was appointed Director of the Office of International Visitor Programs (CU/IVP) in the Bureau of Educational and Cultural Affairs. CU/IVP was the office that conducted the International Visitor Program (IVP), now called International Visitor Leader Program (IVLP), which brings foreign leaders to the United States for periods of one week to one month for familiarization and meetings with professional colleagues. At that time, it brought some 2,000 people to the United States each year from all over the world.[3]

The IVP has been consistently rated by American ambassadors as the most effective program in the State Department's panoply of exchanges. It began on a large scale after World War II in occupied Germany and Japan as the Foreign Leader Program, and grantees came as individuals on programs designed to meet their specific needs and interests. Grants were initially for ninety days, and visitors often made coast-to-coast tours of the United States. As time became more important, and the selected leaders more prominent, the length of stay was shortened, first to sixty days and then to thirty. During my tenure in CU/IVP I shortened it further—seven to ten days for high-level people who could not be away for longer periods of time

Visitors were met on arrival in the United States by officers of the State Department Reception Centers—in those years in New York, Miami, New Orleans, San Francisco, Los Angeles, and Honolulu—facilitated through immigration and customs, and assisted in making their connecting flights or rail travel. In Washington they met with one of the program agencies under contract to the State Department, where travel itineraries and appointments were made according to the needs and interests of each visitor. At that time there were three such program agencies—the Governmental Affairs Institute, the Institute of International Education, and the Department of Labor (which handled labor grantees).

Tying all this together, and ensuring its success, was one of those remarkable American volunteer organizations, Community Services to International Visitors (COSERV), a network of locally-funded community organizations across the country. Since 1982 it has been known as National Council for International Visitors (NCIV), and its more than 80,000 volunteers practice Public Diplomacy by arranging programs in ninety-two communities throughout the United States, escorting the visitors to their professional appointments, and arranging hospitality in American homes. In 2006 NCIV organized 11,777 local programs for International Visitors and 7,318 local programs

---

[3] Today, the International Visitor Leadership Program brings more than 4,000 visitors to the United States each year.

for other exchangees.[4] Among the future luminaries welcomed in the past by COSERV and NCIV local chapters were Tony Blair, Margaret Thatcher, Anwar Sadat, Giscard d'Estaing, Indira Ghandi, Julius Nyerere, and F.W. de Klerk, long before they became important political figures in their home countries.

Soviet visitors had been coming to the United States under the cultural agreement since 1958, and for some of them—political leaders, writers, journalists, and others—their costs had been covered by the International Visitors Program. But they had been coming in groups, with a leader, and often a KGB "minder," rather than as individuals. In the periodic renegotiation of the cultural agreement, the Soviets had consistently rejected language proposed by the State Department that people be exchanged "in groups or as individuals." In one negotiation, when the US side once more proposed to add the word "individuals," the Soviet negotiator explained to us, with a straight face, that they had no individuals in the Soviet Union.

To accustom the Soviets to send people as individuals, I came up with a simple idea. The State Department had been planning to initiate "multiregional" projects—groups of International Visitors from various countries around the world who were all interested in one timely issue.[5] Rather than have an escort-interpreter for each International Visitor, there would be considerable savings in having only two for a group of eighteen to twenty people from different countries. Also, a better program, with more meetings with high-level American experts, could be arranged for a group than for an individual. In addition, the foreign participants could exchange information among themselves on how their countries were facing the same problem.

The first such multiregional project was on environmental protection. When the Soviets were invited to participate and learned that their nominee would participate as an equal with others in the group, they readily agreed to join the project. The ice had been broken, and they participated with regularity in future multiregionals. And we learned that the Soviet Union did indeed have individuals.

---

[4] Because some visitors travel to more than one community, some are counted more than once.

[5] Credit for conceiving the idea of multiregional programs goes to Dean Mahin who was then with the Governmental Affairs Institute.

Jousting with the Jewish Defense League

The United States had a terrorist threat long before al Qaeda, and it was known as the Jewish Defense League (JDL). Founded in 1968 by Meir Kahane, an ordained rabbi, to teach Jews to defend themselves, it soon took on a new mission—to protest the Soviet Union's treatment of its Jews. Among the JDL's tactics to draw attention to the plight of Soviet Jewry were physical attacks on Soviet diplomatic missions and personnel, and disruption of performances by Soviet performing artists in the United States. The JDL actions against visiting Soviet artists included releasing stink bombs in crowded performance halls, throwing blood on performing artists, and releasing marbles to trip up skaters in Soviet ice shows. The recklessness of such actions reached a climax on 26 January 1972, when the JDL smoke bombed the New York offices of impresario Sol Hurok, causing the death of one Hurok employee, a Jewish woman, and injuries to thirteen other Hurok staffers.

One year later, we learned that the JDL was planning to disrupt the opening performance at Washington's Kennedy Center of a US tour by a Ukrainian folk dance group. The US government was especially concerned because Soviet Minister of Culture Furtseva would be in Washington and planned to attend the performance. But preventive measures were taken and the performance was not disrupted.

Mme Furtseva had a grand time on her American tour, including shopping in New York City where a Russian-speaking State Department woman officer was assigned to escort her. At Macy's department store, they started at the top floor and worked their way down to the ground floor, with the Minister buying everything in sight that she liked, including a wig. As Karl Marx might have said, "To each according to her needs."

Soviet Exchanges

After a year at CU/IVP, in another round of musical chairs I was appointed director of the Office of Soviet and East European Exchanges (CU/EE) in the Bureau of Educational and Cultural Affairs. The longtime director of that office, Guy Coriden, had been sent to Geneva as a member of the US delegation to the

Conference on Security and Cooperation in Europe (CSCE), and I was delighted to replace him.

CU/EE conducted the State Department's exchanges with the Soviet Union and Eastern Europe, for which in those years it had an annual budget of some five million dollars, exclusive of performing arts. That may not seem like a princely sum today, but in those days costs were much lower and a dollar went much further.

Roughly half of the annual budget went for exchanges with the Soviet Union, most of them obligations under the cultural agreement, and the other half to Eastern Europe—Poland, Hungary, Czechoslovakia, Yugoslavia, Romania, and Bulgaria. A portion of the budget was also reserved for "Cooperation with Private Initiative" (CPI), an initiative of Assistant Secretary John Richardson to provide "seed money" to US private institutions that were conducting exchanges with overseas partners. It was Public Diplomacy at a very low cost.

One such grant, for example, went to the State University of New York (SUNY) to help cover some costs of its new exchange with Moscow State University. Another went to Indiana University to help support its Polish Studies Center, established in exchange for a Center of American Studies at Warsaw University. Other grants were awarded to American institutions, often state universities whose regulations prohibited them from spending their own funds for foreign travel. At times professors would come to us explaining that their universities were prepared to initiate an exchange with the Soviet Union but could not use their funds for foreign travel, so could they please have a grant of $1,000 for travel to Moscow for a week to conclude the deal. If we liked the proposal we wrote the grant, although writing a grant for $1,000, as our administrative staff complained, was as time-consuming as writing one for $100,000. But again, it was Public Diplomacy on the cheap.

Our largest grant was to the International Research and Exchanges Board (IREX) which represented the US scholarly community in exchanges with the Soviet Union and Eastern Europe. IREX and its predecessor, the Inter-University Committee on Travel Grants (IUCTG), had originally been funded by the Ford Foundation and the participating American universities that waived their costs for Soviet students and scholars. State Department funding for IUCTG began with a grant of $10,500 in 1959, to enable the first group of Soviet students under the cultural agreement to spend a few weeks traveling around the United States at the end of their studies. Over the years, State funding gradually increased, but it took a quantum leap during the 1970s when Ford reduced its funding of international programs. As a consequence, State began to fund more than half of the IREX budget, with other federal funds coming from the US Office of Education and the National Endowment for the Humanities. With those federal funds we were able to fulfill our obligations for scholarly exchanges under the US-Soviet cultural agreement.

The Graduate Student/Young Faculty (GS/YF) exchange of IREX was considered the flagship of our educational and scholarly exchanges with the Soviet Union. On the US side, it consisted of graduate students who were doing research for their doctoral dissertations, and young faculty members who already had their doctorates. In the early years of the exchanges, most of the Americans were in Russian language, literature, and history, because the Soviets in those years would rarely accept students in other academic disciplines. On the Soviet side, most of the GS/YF were older, already had their *Kandidat* degree, roughly equivalent to our PhD, and were mostly in various fields of science and technology.

During the negotiation of the first cultural agreement, President Eisenhower, who actively promoted people-to-people exchanges and contacts, considered inviting 10,000 Soviet students to the United States and paying all their expenses without requiring numerical reciprocity. The idea even had the approval of FBI Director J. Edgar Hoover, but the State Department, at the time, was trying to get the Soviets to agree to exchange 100 students, and it believed that Eisenhower's proposal for 10,000 would frighten them and would certainly be rejected. Eventually, the Soviets agreed to exchange only twenty students each year, although in the first year they withdrew three of their nominees, and only seventeen arrived for study. In response, the United States was obliged to also withdraw three of its nominees.

Over the years, US negotiators consistently tried to increase the number of graduate students and young faculty to be exchanged, but progress was slow. The Soviets eventually agreed to twenty-five, then thirty, and finally fifty, but that was the highest number ever reached under the cultural agreement.

A Tale of Two Justices

Travel to Moscow was very popular during the détente years, and everyone wanted to get on board, including Chief Justice Warren Burger. Burger liked to travel abroad during the court's summer recess and confer with other chief justices. But because federal judges do not have funds for foreign travel, Burger would try to get other agencies to support his summer sojourns. So, at a diplomatic reception in Washington, Burger buttonholed Secretary of State William Rogers and persuaded him to fund his mission to Moscow. And since Educational and Cultural Affairs was the only bureau in State with the necessary funds for the Chief Justice's foreign travel, it fell to me to prepare an American Specialist grant for Burger and a staff assistant for travel to Moscow to meet with Lev N. Smirnov, Chairman of the Soviet Supreme Court.

In briefing Burger's staff assistant, I explained that the Soviets would likely offer to pay the costs of their stay in Moscow, an offer that Burger should politely decline since it would prepare the way for a reciprocal visit by Smirnov to the United States. The Soviet judiciary was an arm of the Soviet government, and Smirnov, I pointed out, was in no way the equivalent of our chief justice.

The Burger visit was scheduled for August when all of official Moscow was on vacation, but Smirnov must have been called back to Moscow because he met with Burger and put him up at the Sovietskaya Hotel, an exclusive hostelry for high-ranking visitors. And, as predicted, all of Burger's costs in Moscow were paid by the Soviets, and he, in return, felt obliged to extend an invitation for Smirnov to visit him in Washington. And so it came about that the State Department had to issue a grant to Smirnov under its International Visitor Program.

Smirnov was not well known abroad, although he had been a Soviet assistant prosecutor at the Nuremberg War Crimes Trials. As a judge, he was a loyal servant of the Soviet state, which is probably why he was selected in 1966 to preside at the show trial of Andrei Sinyavsky and Yuli Daniel, the two Russian writers who were sentenced to lengthy stays in work camps for having published "anti-Soviet" works abroad under pseudonyms. Somehow, we survived that embarrassing situation, and Smirnov's visit did not attract attention in Washington.

After five years in the gulag, Sinyavsky was released in 1971 and allowed to emigrate to France, where he was appointed professor of Russian literature at the Sorbonne. When I met him in 1986 at his home near Paris and related the circumstances of Smirnov's visit to the United States, he replied graciously but with obvious satisfaction, "*Nichevo* (it doesn't matter), I outlived him."

But there's a still-happier ending to this story. The old American Specialist program is still functioning at the State Department as the Speakers and Specialists Program, and each year, as a prime example of Public Diplomacy, it sends more than 700 prominent Americans abroad for face-to-face dialogues with people of other countries. And in 2003 one of them was Supreme Court Justice Anthony M. Kennedy, who traveled to Russia.

A Valve Job for a Prominent Playwright

Russians came to the United States for all sorts of reasons under the cultural agreement. Under the terms of the agreement, the sending side nominated its participants, and the receiving side usually accepted them.

For the US side, the State Department tried to find the best-qualified Americans to send, and given the discomforts and stresses associated with a visit to the Soviet Union, we often had to persuade them to go. For the Soviet side, there were other criteria. Some Soviets were nominated because they were the senior persons in their fields, and in a traditional society they had to travel to the United States before anyone else in their institute or field could. Some were nominated as political payoffs—a reward for loyalty to the Communist Party and regime. Others came because they represented a nationality whose turn had come to participate in the exchange. And others simply because they knew the right people. We never knew what or whom to expect.

It was therefore a pleasant surprise when the USSR Ministry of Culture, in the mid-1970s, nominated two well-known stars of the Soviet stage, Oleg Yefremov and Mikhail Roshchin, for a two-week visit to the United States. The two were as different as night and day, but they worked together well as a team.

Yefremov was a renowned actor and the artistic director of MXAT, the Moscow Art Theater, an institution that had a well-deserved reputation as one of the best Moscow theaters. An ethnic Russian, he was outgoing, gregarious, emotional, and full of the Russian soul. Yefremov also had a prodigious appetite for alcohol, and appeared to be under the influence at all hours of the day and night, although it did not seem to impair his performance.

Roshchin was a promising young playwright, as well as theater director. A Jew, he was reserved, reflective, sober, and did not drink at all, and I was to learn the reason why soon after they embarked on their tour of American regional theaters.

A telephone call from Houston one morning informed me that Roshchin was in the operating room of a Houston hospital where Michael DeBakey, the world famous heart surgeon, was replacing his faulty heart valves. That came as a surprise. The Soviets had not told us that Roshchin had a heart problem and needed surgery. Furthermore, surgery with the busy DeBakey was usually scheduled far in advance. It turned out, moreover, that Roshchin had not been formally admitted to the hospital, and how he got into the operating room remains another Russian riddle.

The operation, however, was a success. Roshchin recuperated a few weeks in Houston, and returned to Moscow with new American valves that enabled him to continue his successful career on all cylinders for many more years. And the visit of Yefremov and Roshchin was followed by several exchanges of plays, and their directors, between Russian and American theaters.

But the story does not end here. One month later I received another call from Houston, from a hospital administrator inquiring if the State Department was prepared to pay Roshchin's hospital costs. I replied that we had not known about his heart condition, had not requested the operation, and were not prepared to pay the costs. The administrator then asked if I had any suggestions as to where he might send the bill.

"Send it to Ambassador Dobrynin at the Soviet Embassy," I replied. And that's where the bill ended up. What Dobrynin did with the bill is not known.

Russian Relations

During the détente years, State Department cooperation with the Soviet Embassy's cultural section in Washington became close. We each had an interest in encouraging exchanges and seeing that our public diplomacy efforts were successful. As a consequence, I saw quite a bit of my Soviet embassy counterparts.

Viktor P. Sakovich was Cultural Counselor in the 1970s. He had served earlier in India and was new to the United States, and in the months after his arrival in Washington I helped him on a number of occasions by explaining how things were done here. In true Russian fashion, he reciprocated by giving me several tips that were very helpful to my work in the Soviet Union.

On a visit to Moscow in 1991, after the Soviet Union had collapsed, I looked up Sakovich and took him to lunch. He appeared to be down and out, and confided that he was taking his lunches at the Foreign Ministry cafeteria. In discussing US-Soviet Cold War rivalries, he volunteered a simple statement, "You won."

Also helpful at times was Soviet Embassy Press Counselor Valentin M. Kamenev. He had previously served as Cultural Counselor and had a wide range of contacts in Washington. He and his attractive wife were also active in Washington diplomatic and social circles, and were often featured in the Style Section of the *Washington Post.* Kamenev was reported to be an officer in the GRU, Soviet military intelligence, but that did not stop him from being helpful to us on several occasions. I particularly remember one occasion when we took him to lunch to sound him out on Soviet positions we might expect at upcoming negotiations for renewal of the cultural agreement. Kamenev advised us not to spring surprises or new initiatives on the Soviets during negotiations. That would only delay the negotiations, he added. New ideas, he advised, should be floated informally, in advance of negotiations, to give the Soviets an opportunity to study them and prepare a position. That good advice was very helpful in our future public diplomacy efforts in Moscow.

Chapter 11

USIA + CU = USICA

One of the Carter administration's first moves in its attempt to "streamline" the federal government was the merger, in 1979, of the State Department's Bureau of Educational and Cultural Affairs (CU) into the US Information Agency (USIA), renamed as the US International Communication Agency (USICA).[1] For those who follow such events, it was another chapter in the never-ending controversy over where to house the US government's international information and cultural exchange activities, now known as Public Diplomacy.[2]

Cultural exchanges have a long history at the Department of State. CU was established in 1938 as the Division of Cultural Relations, and elevated to Bureau status in 1957. Scholarly exchanges, often known as the Fulbright Program, were legislated by the Congress in 1947, and the exchange of grantees began the following year. The International Visitor Program, which brings foreign leaders to the United States for visits of one week to a month or more, as well as an American Specialist program that sends prominent Americans abroad, also began in 1938, and the two programs reached full flower in Germany and Japan after World War II.

USIA was created by the Eisenhower administration in 1953 as a weapon in the Cold War to explain and support Ameri-

---

[1] Reorganization Plan No. 2 (10 April 1979).

[2] For a detailed history of this controversy, see Richard T. Arndt, *The First Resort of Kings: American Cultural Diplomacy in the Twentieth Century* (Washington, D.C.: Potomac Books, Inc., 2005).

can foreign policy and promote US national interests through overseas information programs; its mission, as its motto succinctly stated, was "Telling America's Story to the World." But through its publications, work with foreign media, and radio broadcasts of the Voice of America, USIA continued the propaganda activities of the World War II Office of War Information (OWI). The decision to put information programs into a new and separate agency was due, in part, to Secretary of State John Foster Dulles, who believed that diplomats should not have operational responsibilities. In 1982, the Reagan administration, reflecting dissatisfaction with the USICA name tag, changed it back to USIA.

In one respect, the merger of CU and USIA made sense. USIA's posts abroad were the overseas arm of both USIA and CU. They did the information work of USIA but also administered the State Department's academic exchanges, performing arts presentations, and International Visitor Program. Educational exchanges, however, were under the purview of the Board of Foreign Scholarships, an advisory body of scholars that valued its independence and did not look kindly on academic exchanges being run by a propaganda agency of the US government. To make matter worse, USICA provided a bonanza for communist media around the world, which noted the similarity between the acronyms ICA and CIA.

Two other difficulties arose in combining CU and USIA. The basic tenet of the Smith-Mundt Act of 1948, which provided legislative authority for the State Department's cultural exchanges, was to increase mutual understanding between Americans and people of other nations.[3] Mutual understanding was also one of the objectives of the Fulbright-Hays Act of 1961.[4] But the "mutuality" aspect troubled some USIA officers, who preferred to focus on influencing other nations, and didn't care much about informing the American public of the world beyond our borders.

The other problem was CU's emphasis on "Cooperation with Private Initiative," the pet project of Assistant Secretary of State John Richardson, who believed that a portion of the CU budget should go to providing "seed money" for exchange programs conducted by private US organizations. Some USIA

---

[3] Public Law 402, 80th Congress.

[4] Public Law 87-256, 87th Congress.

officers, however, were skeptical about funding such private initiatives, and preferred to maintain full control over their resources.

To assist USICA in coping with its new responsibilities for overseeing educational and cultural exchanges with the Soviet Union and Eastern Europe, and in negotiating cultural agreements with those countries, a new position was created for me at USICA—Deputy Assistant Director for Europe (Exchanges)—with responsibility for exchanges with both Western and Eastern Europe. In that position I represented USICA in the negotiation of the renewal of exchange agreements with the Soviet Union and Romania, before retiring in January 1980.

Twenty-one years later, on 1 October 1998, during the second Clinton administration, the State Department buckled under pressure from Senator Jesse Helms, the North Carolina Republican who had become Chairman of the Foreign Relations Committee, and merged USIA into the Department of State, with the new organization to be headed by an Undersecretary for Public Diplomacy and Public Affairs. The result, however, has been disappointing since the whole has been less than the sum of its parts, and US Public Diplomacy efforts were overwhelmed by the anti-American sentiment that increased around the world during the first and second George W. Bush administrations. As of this writing, it remains to be seen what the next administration will do in the continuing game of reorganizing the Public Diplomacy efforts of the federal government.

Whatever is decided—and as in the past, there are many views on what should be done—the White House, Congress, and the public at large hopefully have now recognized that Public Diplomacy, with both its cultural and information components, should be an important element in US foreign relations.

Chapter 12

HELSINKI AND HUMAN RIGHTS

The participating States ... make it their aim to facilitate freer movement and contacts, individually and collectively, whether privately
or officially, among persons, institutions and organizations of the
participating States, and to contribute to the solution of the hu-
manitarian problems that arise in that connexion....

–Helsinki Final Act

After thirty years in the Foreign Service, I retired in January
1980 at age fifty-six. With my promotion to a management position as a USIA Deputy Assistant Director, I had become bored
with budgets, pestered with personnel problems, and addled
by administrative affairs. I also did not look forward, after a
change of administrations, to briefing a new round of political
appointees on the realities of foreign affairs and the details of
dealing with the Russians.

A few months spent at home were restful—reading, garden-
ing, jogging, and napping—until I got a call from R. Spencer
Oliver, Executive Director of the Commission on Security and
Cooperation in Europe, inviting me to join the Commission as
a staff consultant. The Helsinki Commission, as it is commonly
called, was established by the US Congress in 1976 to monitor
implementation of the Final Act of the Conference on Security
and Cooperation in Europe (CSCE), signed the previous year in
Helsinki, Finland.

The signing in Helsinki by thirty-three European heads of
state or government, as well as the Prime Minister of Canada
and the President of the United States, had evoked considerable

debate and drama. Not since the Congress of Vienna in 1815, which redrew the map of Europe and established a peace that lasted forty years, had so many European leaders assembled to put their pens to a paper outlining future relations between their states. Although not a treaty and not legally binding, the Helsinki Final Act, as the conference's concluding document is known, was a political statement that its signatories pledged to observe.[1]

The Final Act recognized, for the first time in an international agreement, respect for human rights and fundamental freedoms, including the freer movement of people, ideas, and information. That recognition was to produce profound change in the Soviet Union.

A European security conference had been proposed by the Soviets in 1954 as surrogate for a World War II peace treaty. Soviet motives were obvious—recognition of postwar borders in Europe (especially Poland's borders with the German Democratic Republic and the Soviet Union), cooperation among European states, reduction of armaments, and removal of foreign (i.e., US) troops from Europe. Under the Soviet proposal, the United States and Canada would have been excluded from the conference.

The Europeans—the neutrals and nonaligned, as well as NATO members—were interested in such a conference, tempted as they were by the prospects for peace and stability in Europe, as well as increased East-West trade. The NATO nations, however, stipulated that their non-European allies, the United States and Canada, must also participate in the conference. In addition, as the preliminary political positioning evolved in the late 1960s, the West Europeans insisted that the conference should also discuss fundamental human rights, including the freer movement of people, ideas, and information.

US reaction to the conference proposal, however, was decidedly cool. Henry Kissinger, as National Security Adviser and later Secretary of State, was not enthusiastic about CSCE, fearing that its focus on human rights would be an impediment to reaching agreement with the Soviet Union on security and other major foreign policy issues, and could complicate US

---

[1] In these pages on CSCE, the author has drawn in part from William Korey, *The Promises We Keep: Human Rights, the Helsinki Process, and American Foreign Policy* (New York: St. Martin's Press, 1993), Prologue and Chapter 1.

efforts to coordinate the responses of our allies to Soviet challenges. Accordingly, instructions to the US delegation to the conference were to support our allies but not be confrontational with the Soviets.

Also skeptical about the conference were East European ethnic groups in the United States that were opposed to recognition of postwar borders in Eastern Europe and to lending legitimacy to communist rule and Soviet hegemony there. But President Nixon had been meeting with Leonid Brezhnev at summit meetings in the early 1970s, and the administration could hardly object to Europeans also wanting to sit at the table with the Soviets and discuss common interests. So the United States participated in the CSCE deliberations, although, reflecting Kissinger's caution, it played a secondary role and left the heavy lifting to its NATO allies.

After three years of extended and arduous negotiations in Helsinki and Geneva, the CSCE reached agreement in 1975 on a forty-page, 40,000-word document. The Soviets got their inviolability of borders, but had to accept language recognizing respect for human rights and fundamental freedoms, as well as the freer movement of people, ideas, and information.

As the date approached for signing the Final Act, domestic opposition in the United States mounted. Although the Final Act was a political statement rather than a treaty and not legally binding, East European émigrés and conservatives in both US political parties strongly criticized the document as a sellout to the Soviets. Governor Ronald Reagan of California, in an early version of his "evil-empire" posture, urged President Gerald Ford not to sign, as did Democratic Senator Henry Jackson of Washington. Mail to the White House ran heavily against signing, and much of the media agreed. The *Wall Street Journal,* in an editorial titled "Jerry, Don't Go," urged the President not to go to Helsinki, charging that CSCE was "purely symbolic, and the symbol is one of Soviet hegemony in Eastern Europe."[2] *The New York Times* called it "a misguided and empty trip."[3]

Ford courageously defied domestic disapproval, flew to Finland, and signed the Helsinki Accords, as they came to be known, and in doing so did as much, if not more, to bring about the collapse of communism than Ronald Reagan did years later.

---

[2] *Wall Street Journal,* 21 July 1975.
[3] *New York Times,* 27 July 1975.

In the following years, the opposition that had been so stri-
dent turned to broad support as the Accords were embraced
by human-rights activists in the Soviet Union, Eastern and
Western Europe, and the United States. Even the staunchest
opponents of the Helsinki process eventually came to regard
it as a useful tool for prodding the Soviets to acknowledge, in
an international accord, the right of nations to protest human
rights violations in other countries. As former CIA Director
Robert M. Gates, a career analyst of the Soviet Union (and current Secretary of Defense), put it:

> CSCE was perhaps the most important early milestone on the path
> of dramatic change inside the Soviet empire. The most eloquent
> testimonials to its importance come from those who were on the
> inside, who began their political odyssey to freedom at that time,
> and who became the leaders of free countries in Eastern Europe in
> 1989.... The human rights issue struck at the very legitimacy and
> survival of the Soviet political structure.[4]

In addition to monitoring compliance with the Final Act,
the founders of the Helsinki Commission had a secondary purpose—to ensure that the United States would continue to support the provisions of the Final Act. With Kissinger's lukewarm
endorsement in mind, Congress created the commission, composed initially of six senators and six representatives (later
increased to nine and nine), and one official each from the Departments of State, Defense, and Commerce. In practice, however, State, Defense, and Commerce participation has been
perfunctory, and the commission has functioned as a committee of Congress. Housed and funded by Congress, it holds hearings, issues reports, monitors Final Act implementation by the
signatories, and has become a popular body for its congressional members. For up-and-coming politicians, it provides
exposure to foreign affairs, as well as a public platform for responding to constituents' complaints, be they religious freedom, reunification of families, freedom to travel, or other basic
human rights.

The prime mover in establishing the Helsinki Commission
was the late Rep. Dante B. Fascell, a Florida Democrat, who

---

[4] Robert M. Gates, *From the Shadows: The Ultimate Insider's Story of Five Presidents and How They Won the Cold War* (New York: Simon and Schuster, 1996)
89–90.

became its first chairman. "The Helsinki process," as it was called, got a further boost in 1983 when Fascell became chairman of the House Foreign Affairs Committee. Under his leadership the commission represented a truly bipartisan effort. A kind and considerate man to work for, when I drafted my first letter for Fascell in response to a constituent's query, he took the trouble to call and compliment me on my draft, adding that it was "just right." (No one at the State Department had ever commended my work. At State, your work was *expected* to be first rate.) Fascell also found the time to visit the commission staff from time to time, and just sit and chat with us over coffee.

I took the Helsinki Commission job with one condition. I wanted to work part time, and I promised Oliver that I would give him eight hours of work in five hours, and at half pay. And I did exactly that, in exchange for a prized parking place on Capitol Hill.

The job also got me two trips to Madrid in 1983 as a member of the US delegation to the CSCE review talks held there, which were nearing their end. Meetings of the conference were closed to the press, but it was my job, as press spokesman for the US delegation, to practice Public Diplomacy by briefing the press after each meeting.

For the almost daily meetings, the thirty-five delegates and their deputies sat around a huge oval table, with other delegation members as backbenchers. I would take notes on what seemed significant and might be released to the press. Immediately after each session, I would conduct a little standup press conference in the foyer of the conference room where, surrounded by representatives of the international media, in another example of Public Diplomacy I would read from my notes and answer questions, thus ensuring that the proceedings of the day's "closed" meetings were made public. Other delegations also held press briefings, but ours were usually the best attended.

NATO caucuses were another interesting aspect of the Madrid meeting. After the conference sessions, and often during the day, the fifteen NATO delegates—including Spain, our host but not yet a member—would caucus to discuss the day's events and make plans for future deliberations. Since NATO works by consensus—all members must agree before a position is taken—it was interesting to observe the doings of the delegates as they maneuvered to come to a consensus. Such meetings, of course, were not public, and there were no briefings for the press.

Max M. Kampelman, our delegation chairman, was an especially able leader, and it is largely due to his skill and tenacity that the Madrid meeting, after three years, concluded with language that considerably expanded the observance of human rights in the signatory states.

Kampelman had an interesting and unusual background. He had received a thorough Jewish religious schooling at a New York yeshiva, but later found his metier in law and political science. He had worked with the labor movement, taught at a university and college, served as staffer to Senator Hubert Humphrey, practiced law in Washington, and participated in numerous political and civic activities. A life-long liberal and anti-communist, he had served as a conscientious objector (CO) during World War II, but in 1955, when no longer a CO, he accepted a commission in the Marine Corps Reserve.[5] And although he was a Democrat, Kampelman served both Republican and Democratic presidents.[6]

Max, as he was known to all, came to the chairmanship of the US delegation to the Madrid CSCE review meeting by default. The Carter administration had initially appointed William Scranton, a former Republican governor of Pennsylvania, and Kampelman as cochairs of the delegation. When Scranton resigned for health reasons, he was replaced by former Attorney General Griffin B. Bell, a distinguished Georgia judge and close friend of President Carter. After Ronald Reagan was elected president in November 1979, both Bell and Kampelman submitted their resignations, as is customary for ambassadors and other presidential appointees. Kampelman, however, was reappointed by Reagan as the sole US chairman at Madrid.

Deputies to Kampelman were Warren Zimmerman, and R. Spencer Oliver. Zimmerman, an able and experienced career Foreign Service Officer, had served in the Soviet Union, understood the workings of the State Department, and later was US

---

[5] Here, I have drawn from Max M. Kampelman, *Entering New Worlds: The Memoirs of a Private Man in Public Life* (New York: HarperCollins, 2001).

[6] Kampelman later, in the Reagan administration, served as head of the US delegation to negotiations with the Soviet Union on nuclear and space arms, and as Counselor at the State Department.

ambassador to Yugoslavia. Oliver, a staff aide to Fascell and Executive Director of the Helsinki Commission, was wily in the ways of bridging differences, and an experienced practitioner in getting things done. During the second year of the Madrid meeting, Zimmerman was replaced by Edward Killham, whose tours of duty in Moscow and at NATO served him well at CSCE.

I recall one incident at Madrid when Oliver literally stole the show from senior diplomats. At a plenary session held in a large amphitheater hall, differences emerged between the NATO and Warsaw Pact delegations. As delegation chairmen were debating the issue on the stage of the hall, Oliver rose from his chair in the audience and walked over and consulted with the NATO group. As the entire hall followed his every move, Oliver next went to the neutrals and consulted there for a few minutes. With compromise language obviously in hand, Oliver then consulted with the Soviet delegation. A few minutes later, compromise language, proposed by one of the neutrals, was unanimously adopted.

Our sojourn in Spain was not all work. Madrid was a pleasant place for a conference. The Spaniards were good hosts, the food was good and the wine inexpensive, although Americans found it difficult to adjust to the Spanish custom of restaurants not serving dinner until 10 p.m. Weekends were free, and the excellent Spanish rail system facilitated visits to the great sites of Spain—Toledo, Granada, Cordoba, Salamanca, and Avila. Only a few years after the passing of the Franco regime, it was also interesting to see Spain going through its own transition to democracy, including an attempted military coup while I was there. One of the more interesting sites was the swimming pool on the roof of the hotel in which the US delegation was housed where, according to the practice common in many European countries at the time, but new to Spain, women went topless.

During the final week of the three-year-long meeting, when a final document had been agreed to, we had a visit by Secretary of State George Shultz. Kampelman planned to give a lunch for Shultz, and asked me to prepare a seating plan. No problem, I thought, since I had prepared many a dinner seating plan for ambassadors, applying the well known rules of protocol as to who sat where and next to whom. But this lunch was different. Not only did we have Americans who had to be seated according to rank, but also our Spanish hosts and NATO colleagues.

It was a tough assignment, but with the help of Max everyone was seated correctly and no one's feelings were hurt.

My three years at the Helsinki Commission were an added fillip to my Foreign Service career, enabling me to learn how the US Congress functioned. It was an experience every senior federal employee should have. And we put the spotlight on human rights. As Kampelman has described it:

> No one had expected much when we began, but, over three years, with persistence, cooperation from our allies, and the desire or need of the Soviets to reach agreement, we had done exceedingly well in placing human rights firmly on the world agenda as it had not been for decades or perhaps forever.[7]

Further gains in human rights were achieved at the Vienna CSCE Review Meeting in 1989, but by then another unexpected telephone call had taken me elsewhere on my Cold War odyssey.

---

[7] Kampelman, *Entering New Worlds,* 285.

Chapter 13

Doing Democracy at NED

In early 1984, while still at the Helsinki Commission, I received a telephone call from John Richardson, board chairman of the newly established National Endowment for Democracy (NED). Richardson, for whom I had worked at the State Department when he was Assistant Secretary for Educational and Cultural Affairs, asked if I would come crosstown to NED for thirty days and show them how to write grants. NED, he explained, was almost halfway through its first fiscal year with a budget of $18.5 million, but had not yet written one grant in support of democracy overseas. Richardson had cleared his request beforehand with Spencer Oliver, my boss at the Helsinki Commission, who had readily given his approval. How those thirty days became eight years is the story of this chapter.

NED is a private non-profit organization created in 1983 to strengthen democratic institutions around the world through non-governmental efforts. With funding from the US Congress, NED makes grants to private groups in the United States who work in partnership with organizations and individuals abroad seeking to promote democracy in their countries.

NED was founded at the initiative of a small group of Washington insiders who believed that the United States needed a "quango" (quasi-autonomous non-governmental organization) to promote democracy and counter communist influence abroad, and that it should be done openly. Among the founders were Rep. Dante Fascell, Sen. William Brock, AFL-CIO President Lane Kirkland, and congressional staffer George Agree. Funded by Congress but operated as a non-governmental agency, NED has four core grantee institutes—the Free Trade Union Institute of the AFL-CIO, representing labor; the Center for International Private Enterprise of the US Chamber of Commerce, for business; and the National Democratic Institute and International Republican Institute, representing the two political parties.[1]

With such a broad constituency, congressional approval and funding was assured, and with strong support from the Reagan White House for a war of ideas with the Soviet Union, the future of NED seemed certain. As President Reagan had presciently predicted in an address to the British Parliament on 8 June 1982, "A march of freedom and democracy will leave Marxism-Leninism on the ash heap of history."[2] Moreover, NED was another exercise in Public Diplomacy, talking directly with the people of other countries.

My first task at NED was to sort through a stack of applications for grants from various US organizations seeking to support democracy in far-flung corners of the world. I was on familiar ground evaluating applications for projects in the Soviet Union, Eastern Europe, and Asia, but there were also requests for funding in Latin America, Africa, and the Middle East, where I had not previously served or even visited. Nevertheless, I was able to help establish procedures for evaluating the proposals, and had a number of them prepared for approval at the next quarterly meeting of the NED board.

Board meetings were always exciting. One participant called it "the best show in town," as the merits of the various proposals for funding were passionately debated by liberals and conservatives, Republicans and Democrats, business and labor.

Among the many distinguished board members during my years at NED were William E. Brock III, Republican Senator from Tennessee and former Secretary of Labor; Frank J. Fahrenkopf, Chairman, Republican National Committee; Dante B. Fascell, Democratic Representative from Florida; Orrin G. Hatch, Republican Senator from Utah; Lane Kirkland, President, AFL-CIO; Henry Kissinger, former Secretary of State; Charles T. Manatt,

---

[1] For more on NED's early years, see Thomas Carothers, "The NED at 10," *Foreign Affairs,* no. 95, Summer 1994, 123–38. For NED's origins, see http://www.ned.org/about/nedhistory.html.

[2] http://millercenter.virginia.edu/scripps/diglibrary/prezspeeches/reagan/rwr_1982_0608.html

Chairman, Democratic National Committee; Walter F. Mondale, former Vice President; Claiborne Pell, Democratic Senator from Rhode Island; Albert Shanker, President, American Federation of Teachers; Charles H. Smith Jr., businessman from Cleveland; and Jay Van Andel, a co-founder of Amway.

Carl Gershman became NED president—actually chief executive officer—on 30 April 1984. Previously, he had been Senior Counselor to Jeanne Kirkpatrick at the US Mission to the United Nations, where he had met many of the players in the political and ideological battles that took place in that international forum. In that capacity, he also served as US Representative to the UN's Third Committee, which dealt with human rights issues, and as Alternate US Representative to the UN Security Council. Prior to his work at the United Nations, Gershman had been a Resident Scholar at Freedom House (1980–1981) and Executive Director of Social Democrats, USA (1974–1980). Gershman was new to Washington and its ways, but with his keen mind, staunch stamina, and bulldog tenacity, he soon mastered the intricacies of the job. When he offered me a permanent position as Program Officer, I readily accepted.

NED was a good place to practice Public Diplomacy. We had a steady stream of visitors from all over the world who were eager to discuss conditions in their home countries and submit requests for funding. NED also kept me in touch with Soviet and Eastern European dissidents, and it introduced me to a number of movers and shakers in Washington. In addition, I was able to negotiate half-time status which enabled me to pursue my writing interests.

In those years, however, NED lacked a geographic focus. Rather than concentrate its limited resources in a few key countries, it attempted to cover the world. The result was a presence in many countries but without a meaningful impact in most of them. Exceptions were Poland and the Soviet Union, which were given high priority in NED's early years.

NED can indeed be proud of the millions of dollars it pumped into Poland to help sustain the Solidarity movement and its underground activities during the martial law crackdown of the early 1980s, as well as the assistance NED provided to democratic movements in other Eastern European countries. But it is fair to ask what lasting results can be shown for the millions spent in the Soviet Union, mainly by the Democratic and Republican Party institutes, to encourage the formation of political parties that failed to find support among the vast majority of the Russian people and did not win a single seat in the parliamentary election of December 2003. Moreover, Russian recipients of NED funding were not able to prevent the rise to power of Vladimir Putin and his coterie of former KGB and military officers, who have stalled and, in many ways, reversed the movement for democracy in Russia. Was it wise to expect that Americans could bring change to such a vast, divisive, and complex country as Russia? Will similar well-intentioned efforts succeed in bringing democracy to the Middle East? Our experience in the Soviet Union shows how difficult it can be to bring democracy to countries that have never known democracy.

AFTERWORD

Will similar public diplomacy practices succeed in the twenty-first century? Can what worked to defeat communism in the twentieth century serve as a model for defeating terrorism and anti-Americanism in the much different world we live in today? Time will tell, but while our experience in the Soviet Union and other communist countries shows how difficult it can be to bring change to other countries, it also shows that patience can pay off.

Stalin died in 1953, but it took more than thirty years for the system he established to be overturned. And that did not happen until a new Soviet generation had come to power, a generation that had been exposed to the world beyond Soviet borders and had come to realize that their media had not been telling them the truth, that communism had failed them, and that the Soviet Union had fallen far behind the West.

To be sure, no two regions of the world are alike, and what worked in the Soviet Union and Eastern Europe in the past may not work in the Middle East today. We now live in a much different world with an explosion of information, thanks to computers, the internet, and satellite television, but we can still employ some of the public diplomacy activities that proved their worth in the past. Here are a few of them that are worth continuing.

Exchanges of people—students, teachers, scholars, scientists and engineers, writers, and political leaders—enable others to see their own countries in a different light and motivate them to work for change. Information activities—radio, televi-

sion, and the printed word—expose millions to the world beyond their country's borders. Exhibitions prove the proverb
that seeing is believing. Performing arts exchanges showcase
country cultures and stimulate creativity in the arts. Much as
athletes need international competition to sharpen their performance, creative artists, as well as scientists, need to exchange ideas with their colleagues in other countries. Support
for English teaching increases the number of people who can
converse with Americans and others face-to-face and without
the assistance of interpreters.

In our attempt to reach foreign audiences, it behooves us
to continue what we know works, but also to be prepared to
use the new technologies. Security challenges alone—the need
to protect participants in Public Diplomacy—should make us
rethink our mix of activities in some countries.

Public Diplomacy, however, should not be an exclusive
preserve of the US government. As in our exchanges with the
Soviet Union, we should encourage participation by the various elements of civil society—our universities, scientific and
medical institutions, professional organizations, human rights
advocates, athletic associations, and individual Americans.

But above all, policy makers should be made aware of the
public opinion consequences of their decisions, abroad as
well as at home. Additional funding and personnel for Public
Diplomacy alone will not win support for American actions.
Those who are expected to practice Public Diplomacy should
have some input to policy decisions. As Edward R. Murrow,
the well-known TV journalist and former director of USIA put
it, they have to be "in on the take-offs and not just the crash
landings."

SELECTED BIBLIOGRAPHY

Arndt, Richard T. *The First Resort of Kings: American Cultural Diplomacy in the Twentieth Century.* Washington, D.C.: Potomac Books, Inc., 2005.

Bassow, Whitman. *The Moscow Correspondents: From John Reed to Nicholas Daniloff.* New York: William Morrow and Co., 1988.

Beam, Jacob D. *Multiple Exposure: An American Ambassador's Unique Perspective on East-West Issues.* New York: W.W. Norton and Co., 1978.

Byrnes, Robert F. *Soviet-American Academic Exchanges, 1958–1975.* Bloomington: Indiana University Press, 1976.

Carothers, Thomas. "The NED at 10." *Foreign Affairs,* no. 95, Summer 1994.

A Country Study: Laos. Washington, D.C.: Federal Research Division, Library of Congress. http://lcweb2.loc.gov/frd/cs/latoc.html

Cousins, Norman. "Tale of Two Exhibitions." *Saturday Review of Literature,* 1 August 1959.

Critchlow, James. *Radio Hole-in-the-Head/Radio Liberty: An Insider's Story of Cold War Broadcasting.* Washington, D.C.: The American University Press, 1995.

Cultural Diplomacy and the National Interest. Washington, D.C.: The Curb Center for Art, Enterprise, and Public Policy at Vanderbilt, 2005.

Dizard, Jr., Wilson P. *Inventing Public Diplomacy: The Story of the U.S. Information Agency.* Boulder, CO: Lynne Rienner Publishers, 2004.

Dobbins, James, et al. *America's Role in Nation-Building: From Germany to Iraq.* Santa Monica, CA: Rand Corporation, 2003.

Heil, Jr., Alan L. *Voice of America: A History.* New York: Columbia University Press, 2003.

Kampelman, Max M. *Entering New Worlds: The Memoirs of a Private Man in Public Life.* New York: Harper Collins, 1991.

Kellerman, Henry J. *Cultural Relations as an Instrument of U.S. Foreign Policy: The Educational Exchange Program Between the United States of America and Germany, 1945–1954.* Washington, D.C.: U.S. Government Printing Office, 1978.

Kiernan, Frances. *Seeing Mary Plain: A Life of Mary McCarthy.* New York: W.W. Norton and Co., 2002.

Korey, William. *The Promises We Keep: Human Rights, the Helsinki Process, and American Foreign Policy.* New York: St. Martin's Press, 1993.

Kreis Resident Officer: Classification Standards Report. Bad Godesberg, Germany: Office of the U.S. High Commissioner for Germany, July 1950.

Kupferberg, Herbert. *The Raised Curtain: Report of the Twentieth Century Fund Task Force on Soviet-American Scholarly and Cultural Exchanges.* New York: Twentieth Century Fund, 1977.

Lewis, Flora. *A Case History of Hope: The Story of Poland's Peaceful Revolution.* New York: Doubleday and Co., 1958.

Littmann, Ulrich. *Partners–distant and close: Notes and footnotes on academic mobility between Germany and the United States of America (1923–1993).* Bonn, Germany: Deutscher Akademischer Austauschdienst, 1997.

Lowe, David. "Ideas to Reality: A Brief History of the National Endowment for Democracy." http://www.ned.org/about/nedhistory.html

Mayers, David. *The Ambassadors and America's Soviet Policy.* New York: Oxford University Press, 1995.

Meeker, Oden. *The Little World of Laos.* New York: Charles Scribner's Sons, 1959.

Newsom, David D., ed. *Private Diplomacy with the Soviet Union.* Lanham, MD: University Press of America, 1987.

Osborne, Milton. *The Mekong: Turbulent Past, Uncertain Future.* New York: Atlantic Monthly Press, 2000.

Paul, Jr., David M. "On the Road Again." *Foreign Service Journal,* March 1987.

Richmond, Yale. *Cultural Exchange and the Cold War: Raising the Iron Curtain.* University Park, PA: Pennsylvania State University Press, 2003.

_____. *US-Soviet Cultural Exchanges, 1958–1986: Who Wins?* Boulder, CO: Westview Press, 1987.

_____. "US-Soviet Cultural Exchanges." *Foreign Service Journal,* December 1990.

_____. "A Tale of Two Georges." *Foreign Service Journal,* October 1992.

_____. "Vientiane, 1954." *Foreign Service Journal,* May 1988.

Robinson, Harlow. *The Last Impresario: The Life, Times, & Legacy of Sol Hurok.* New York: Viking, 1994.

Shaplen, Robert. "Democracy's Best Salesmen in Germany." *Colliers,* 9 February 1952.

Sosin, Gene. *Sparks of Liberty: An Insider's Memoir of Radio Liberty.* University Park, PA: Pennsylvania State University Press, 1999.

Starr, Richard F., ed. *Public Diplomacy: USA Versus USSR.* Stanford, CA: Hoover Institution Press, 1986.

Starr, S. Frederick. *Red and Hot: The Fate of Jazz in the Soviet Union.* New York: Oxford University Press, 1983.

Stieglitz, Perry. *In A Little Kingdom.* Armonk, NY: M. E. Sharpe, Inc., 1990.

Tuch, Hans N. *Communicating with the World: U.S. Public Diplomacy Overseas.* An Institute for the Study of Diplomacy Book. New York: St. Martin's Press, 1990.

"The U.S. – Warts and All: Edward R. Murrow, A Commemorative Symposium." Washington, D.C.: The U.S. Information Agency Alumni Association and The Public Diplomacy Foundation, 1991.

INDEX

Also by Yale Richmond

Cultural Exchange and the Cold War: Raising the Iron Curtain
Into Africa: Intercultural Insights (with Phyllis Gestrin)
From Da to Yes: Understanding the East Europeans
From Nyet to Da: Understanding the Russians
Soviet-American Cultural Exchanges: Ripoff or Payoff?
Hosting Soviet Visitors: A Handbook